Going Vegan 4 Goodness

The Plant-Based and Vegan Way
to Better Health and Humanity

Mark Suarkeo

Foreword by Del Sroufe,
Author of *The New York Times* Bestseller
*Forks Over Knives—The Cookbook: Over 300 Recipes for
Plant-Based Eating All Through the Year*

Going Vegan 4 Goodness

Copyright © 2021 by Mark Suarkeo

All Rights Reserved

Publisher's Legal Disclaimer
This book presents a wide range of opinions about a variety of topics related to social issues, environmental issues, animal welfare, and human health and well-being including educational information related to potentially preventing and reversing certain lifestyle chronic diseases. These opinions reflect the research and ideas of the author or those whose ideas the author presents, but are not intended to substitute for the advice or services of a trained physician, registered dietitian or other professional medical practitioner. Please consult with your primary care physician or other pertinent healthcare practitioner before beginning any kind of new diet, taking any new vitamin, mineral, or supplement or before starting a new exercise routine or program. The author and publisher disclaim responsibility for any adverse effects resulting directly or indirectly from any information contained in this book.

The information in this book is provided for educational purposes only. It is not intended as a substitute for advice from a healthcare professional.

Persons with medical conditions or who are taking medications are encouraged to discuss diet and lifestyle changes with their primary care physician or other pertinent healthcare professional.

Photo credits given in caption where available, and copyrights belong to the respective owners. Uncredited photos used under public domain, sourced from pixabay.com. Images from the Got Milk?® advertising campaign are used under fair use. Got Milk?® is the registered trademark of the California Milk Processor Board.

To my mom, Violeta:

Thank you for all the times you nursed Michael and me
to good, strong health whenever we got sick or suffered
from any kind of pain or injury.

Foreword

By Del Sroufe, author of *The New York Times Bestseller Forks Over Knives—The Cookbook: Over 300 Recipes for Plant-Based Eating All Through the Year*

My first restaurant job was in a vegetarian restaurant close to the Ohio State University where I went to school. It was a 1960's throwback coffee house with a bead shop next door, and the first day I walked in the place, I fell in love with it. It was laid back, and full of eclectic people drinking hazelnut coffee or one of the 60 teas on the beverage menu. The food was amazing and unpretentious and a little bit decadent. We served sandwiches, nachos, quiche, the best chili I've ever had, and daily specials like lasagna. I used to order a cheese melt with double cheese on a bagel. It was literally cheese melted in the microwave oven on a bagel or sandwich bread, topped with lettuce, tomato, onion, mustard and mayonnaise.

I worked there 8-½ years and watched as the restaurant became more vegan friendly, adding dishes like steamed vegetables, brown rice and beans, and a full pastry case of vegan baked goods (created by yours truly) to the menu. I wasn't vegetarian when I started working there but Libby, the owner of the restaurant, used to tell me about the horrors of animal farming, and it eventually got me thinking about my own food choices. In 1997, I became vegan and left the restaurant to open my own vegan bakery.

My transition to a vegan diet was more for the animals than for the health of the environment or my personal health. In fact, I gained 200 pounds on an unhealthy vegan diet, eating processed foods like potato chips and beer (my favorite dinner), vegan pizza made with white flour, cakes and pies and cookies all made with lots of fat, and sugar, and everything cooked in oil. It sure did taste good, but there was nothing healthy about that way of eating.

It took me four years of suffering with 275 pounds of extra body fat to get me to ask for help and doing so changed my life. I started taking classes at The Wellness Forum in Columbus, Ohio and started changing my relationship with food. I learned about calorie density, and the benefits of a whole foods diet to heal the body, and the importance of exercise, rest, and water. It took me 3 years or so, but I lost 200 pounds and kept working to lose the remaining 75 or so.

In 2009, I was interviewed for a documentary, *Forks Over Knives*, and saw my life changed once again. My interview never made it to the big screen, but I was eventually asked to write their first cookbook, *Forks Over Knives - The Cookbook*. The cookbook was on *The New York Times* bestseller's list for 37 weeks. The rest, as they say, is history.

Writing *Forks Over Knives - The Cookbook* opened many doors for me. I have travelled and done public speaking tours, and I've been able to write three more cookbooks. On a personal level, and probably most importantly, through the people I met, I was able to eventually make the connection between my personal health, the health of the communities in which I live, and the health of the planet. Today I work for an organization that seeks to help others to make that connection, The T. Colin Campbell Center for Nutrition Studies.

I tell you some of my story because I had to cobble together much of my knowledge for adopting a healthy diet. *Going Vegan 4 Goodness* would have saved me a lot of research time if it had existed some 25 years ago. Mark Suarkeo's book is a good resource for anyone looking to adopt a plant-based diet. In addition to good recipes, it provides what Mark calls "actionable steps" for going vegan and for understanding the connection between individual, communal, and planetary health. That connection helps remind me every day that my actions have an impact on others and on our planet.

I have two favorite sections in the book: *Section 9*, which answers the question *"Where do you get your protein?"* — a question you will hear again and again once you tell someone you are vegan and *Section 13: Veganizing your favorite dishes*. People are often surprised at how exciting and full of variety the vegan diet is, and Mark's recipe section helps make the case for that argument.

I hope you enjoy Mark's book and I hope you embrace the journey to come once you have read this book.

PREFACE

I can recall the day I saw my first bilateral transtibial (below-knee amputations on both legs) patient. Jasmine was a petite, elderly Asian woman with short black hair and was a bit on the wrinkly side. As I entered the treatment room at UCLA's outpatient Prosthetics & Orthotics Clinic, I first noticed her sitting timidly in her wheelchair. She had a blanket draped over her lap covering her thighs and the remaining parts of her legs. Her cause of amputations: gangrene secondary to type 2 diabetes.

As her Clinical Prosthetist, my primary job was to build Jasmine a pair of comfortable, highly functional prosthetic limbs that would help her feel safe, stable, and confident. As one could imagine after an amputation surgery, her life was never going to be the same, and it wasn't just the physical challenges she had to face. Grief, depression, and low self-esteem were just a few of the emotional and psychological effects she would battle through.

While treating Jasmine, I recalled the shocking statistics I had learned in prosthetics school. Patients with diabetes have a 52 - 80% mortality rate within 5 years of their amputation date.[1] Among a long list of other complications, Jasmine faced a greater risk of systemic infection, heart attack, and of course, demoralizing and debilitating falls. Consequences she could've faced include organ failure, life-threatening blood clots, breathing difficulty, and pressure ulcers from being non-ambulatory (unable to walk without a wheelchair). I also knew that, statistically speaking, her life was considerably shortened. With the help of our rehabilitation team, I needed to get her up walking and accomplishing her activities of daily living in a timely fashion. Jasmine needed hope, encouragement, and a strong sense of self-reliance.

Treating patients like Jasmine who were diagnosed with type 2 diabetes in my early professional career has completely evolved my outlook and influenced a new lifestyle. Nowadays, one of my main goals is to prevent moms and dads alike around the world from suffering what Jasmine and her family went through. While seeking ways to help people prevent diabetes, I learned firsthand that nutrition is a key factor - specifically, a healthy plant-based approach.

Having witnessed Jasmine's physical and psychological struggles wasn't my only motivation to alter my path, though. As a matter of fact, it was my very own mom who inspired me to make the pivotal shift. That's because she had been diagnosed with type 2 diabetes years before. Thinking back, she could've been the Asian woman at the prosthetics clinic sitting in a wheelchair with both feet cut off. To this day, she's currently insulin-dependent, facing similar health risks that Jasmine encountered. Thankfully, I saw that there is a way to help her avoid that potential outcome.

While learning about the healing effects of plant-based foods, I also started to naturally gravitate towards nature, mindfulness practice, and things like polyculture farming. Eventually, I started to make the connection of how our daily food choices can make a lasting impact. It has raised my awareness on how livestock are treated horribly within the animal agriculture industry and it ultimately has shifted my perspective towards veganism. Aside from all the animals and our planet needing our love and care, improving my family's health was my initial reason for going vegan. I'm vegan for all the children in my life, as well for those in yours, too. Our future generations are relying on us. Our aging parents are, too. This is in honor of Jasmine and many of my other past patients who became family to me. In fact, the pages you're about to read are for anyone who can relate to my story and resonate with why I am here with you now.

So, how did I get here with you? I've chosen to live more purposefully and go with the flow of my personal vegan journey. Raising more awareness, particularly for African-Americans, Hispanics and Latinos, Asians and Pacific Islanders, and American Indians is important to me because these groups are known to be at greater risk for developing chronic lifestyle diseases. As a native Thai and Filipino, this is one reason why I am forging on this path myself. I also believe this path is what guided me towards discovering how to help my mom (and maybe yours, too) to live a healthier, higher quality of life.

Mark

INTRODUCTION

Your conscious decision of *Going Vegan 4 Goodness* does a lot more than save dozens of animals' lives per year. Improving the well-being of others while promoting the health and sustainability of our planet are just two good reasons for living a vegan lifestyle. As you set forth in making such a meaningful life change, you'll find yourself discovering even more of the greater goodness that arises from *going vegan*.

This easy to read guidebook is broken down into short sections. You'll come across a range of inter-related topics including how we've been socially conditioned to eat animals, plant-based nutrition basics, and how to start veganizing your favorite dishes. The photo-filled pages are intended to spark intuitive feelings within your mind and heart — and don't worry, you won't see anything gory! My hope is that you will accept the challenge of expanding your perspectives while observing your acquired beliefs, underlying values, and everyday actions related to your daily food choices.

First, you'll read through some of the social and environmental issues linked to animal welfare, animal agriculture, and human health. Setting a foundation and understanding how food (and the food industry) are all connected to your health and our planet is very important. You'll develop a sense of knowing — what's on your plate can spread more goodness yet also support further pain and destruction. You'll also recognize how your actions are especially impactful to our treasured youth whose future will be cleaner, greener, and brighter, thanks to you!

Ready, steady...go take purposeful action!
Throughout the entire book, you'll come across a total *15 Actionable Steps Towards Going Vegan*. These practical acts range from super simple and social media-related to a bit more thought-provoking and entertaining type activities with friends and family. I encourage you to take on each step as they are meant to provide you with an added boost into the world of veganism while keeping it fun, educative, and worthwhile!

You see, *Going Vegan 4 Goodness* isn't just about your health. It's not solely about saving the billions of animals who are innocently killed for food each year, either. It's an understanding that there is a higher purpose to this path you're on right *now*. I believe that you've chosen to read this book because you're called upon to make a difference. Whether it's to lose weight or become healthier, promote animal welfare, help a family member, or any other reason - your unique purpose and the goodness that you already possess within will prove to be beneficial to our world. I am humbly grateful for joining you on this transition as you strive to live life consciously with true intention.

My goal is to help you discover *your* purpose for *going vegan* and show that you can live a healthy vegan *way of life* with tasty culinary satisfaction! If you're reading this because you're vegan-curious wanting to learn more, then this book can certainly help you decide what's best for you. After working as a Clinical Prosthetist at UCLA Medical Center for over a decade and discovering the benefits of eating plant-based, my life changed completely.

My personal mission of treating patients with amputations (mostly due to diabetes and poor lower extremity circulation) turned into helping prevent them from occurring in the first place. I know you have a worthy purpose within you, too.

There's goodness all around

Despite all of the pain, suffering, and destruction that's tied into animal agriculture and human diseases, there is still so much goodness out there in the world. Thankfully, you possess a great deal of it, which the world needs more of. I'm not suggesting that you go out to become the next humanitarian of the century. But who knows? Maybe you're on that path and just don't know it yet! Nevertheless, I do believe that you *can and will* make a meaningful difference and positively change the world for someone special, including yourself. Whatever your own good reason(s) for going vegan may be, I'm glad that you are willfully opening your heart and mind to new possibilities. It all starts with self-awareness and honest acceptance to love your full evolution.

CONTENTS

Section 1 - Making the Transition to Going Vegan

Taking that very first step towards *going vegan 4 goodness* was the first hurdle. Congratulations! I want you to know that you're not alone and you never will be during this exciting time in your life.

Having a support system and group of friends who align with your values, beliefs, and actions is really beneficial during your transition and beyond.

I am grateful to connect with you and I am thankful for all the goodness you're giving back to our world. Let's get started by presenting you with the worldwide, ever-growing vegan community. Checking out a handful of different social media accounts is a really good way to get rolling. Try searching for some local individuals, groups, and organizations in your area too.

Making connections on any social media platform is an easy way to find like-minded vegans in your area and throughout the world.

A Few Suggested Communities on Instagram

@dominionmovement
@earthalliance
@livekindly
@milliondollarvegan
@thehumaneleague
@thesavemovement
@vegancommunity
@veganoutreach
@weareveganuary

Throughout the following pages, you'll learn that preventing certain chronic diseases and losing unhealthy body weight are not the only potential added benefits for going vegan. Eating a plant-based or vegan diet has also been found to be the single biggest way you can reduce your environmental impact on the planet.

Although you'll come across many vegans solely fighting for animal rights, there's so much more to being vegan. Promoting a sustainable planet earth, protecting wildlife, and standing up for other humans facing social injustices are what a typical vegan contributes to the world every single day.

Photo: @genesisbutler_

Actionable Step Towards Going Vegan #1

Search and follow at least 3-5 plant-based and vegan-related Instagram accounts that are most appealing to you. Check out their posts and stories and begin engaging with their content. Explore to see what fits your interests!

Here are a few to check out.

@mercyforanimals is a non-profit based in Los Angeles, CA that is dedicated to eradicating a cruel food system and replacing it with one that is not just kind to animals, but also essential for the future of our planet and all who share it.

@nutrition_facts_org is a noncommercial, non-profit, science-based resource with some really great educational video content providing the latest in evidence-based nutrition.

@vegancommunity is the largest community of vegans from all over the world. Keep up with the rapidly expanding vegan social movement through inspiration, guides, recipes, and tips.

Millions of people all around the world have already made the transition to living a vegan lifestyle. Every single person is unique and has their own personal reasons and timely path towards making their purposeful lifelong change. Whatever your reason may be, you'll soon learn why it's one of the most rewarding and impactful decisions you've ever made.

What does it mean to go vegan?

People who choose to be vegan avoid, as much as possible, all forms of exploitation and cruelty to animals whether for food, clothing, experimentation, entertainment or any other use. Vegans do not eat or use any kind of animal products.

This includes not wearing animal skins and fur (leather, feathers, fur, wool and silk), or using products that have been tested on animals. Vegans do not support or pay for activities or entertainment that exploit animals, either.

The driving change for animal liberation is just one major reason why millions of people are choosing to live a vegan lifestyle. In the following several pages, I will briefly share why going vegan is one of the best things you can do to help end animal cruelty. Together, we can end unnecessary suffering and stop the brutal deaths of billions of animals killed in slaughterhouses every single year.

Section 2 - Animal Liberation

People who identify as being vegan tend to have an emotional connection to the entire animal species. Such individuals share a personal level of compassion and empathy for every kind of being. They particularly stand up for farmed animals who undergo enslavement, torture, and exploitation in today's modern world of factory farming and food production.

Photo: @aimeenoshamee/@thesavemovement

By simply not supporting the animal agriculture industry and choosing plant-based foods over animal-based products, you are making a big difference.

Animals who are used, abused, and exploited for fashion are also a major concern for vegans. Examples are horses, kangaroos and ostriches who are used to make leather. Wool can come from sheep, goats, llamas, alpaca or Tibetan antelope.

Hunting and trapping wild exotic animals such as foxes, minks, beavers, and even seals also result in the inhumane treatment of such animals. This may include shearing, dehorning, and castrating animals while they are still alive.

Sadly, harsh abuse including punching, kicking, electrocuting, forcefully throwing and impregnating animals without regard are also common practices within the meat, dairy, and fur industries.

Whether inflicted on a human or an animal, witnessing any kind of physical harm and/or psychological abuse is an awful experience. Many of us would feel a bit of anxiety or tension if we saw it firsthand. To victimize or mistreat any type of being is simply an unjust and unkind act. Many would agree that basic dignity and respect is deserved by all who share this earth.

No longer buying fashionable items made of animal products such as leather shoes, fur coats, wool blankets, down jackets, or cashmere sweaters decreases the demand for these commercial products.

Boycotting such products will force major brands to stop their mistreatment and exploitation of innocent animals being used and abused for profit.

Society's increase of awareness and stance against what is now considered socially unacceptable will help liberate animals to live wild and free as they are meant be.

Developing a more compassionate outlook and understanding that we are not superior to non-human animals is fundamental to ending such cultural norms and false justification of animal exploitation.

Reflecting upon your attitudes can help you understand Peter Singer's **Principle of Equal Consideration of Interests**, which states that one should never favor the interest of a specific group, race, gender, or species over that of another group, and that a balance of fairness must be evenly weighed when deciding on a moral issue.

Photo: Jo-Anne McArthur/We Animals Media

speciesism: a prejudice or bias against other beings, simply on account of their species.

How did we get this way?

Like many of you, I have learned to show love and affection for certain kinds animals such as our household dogs and cats. Pets become loyal family members and are often treated like another son or daughter or much cuter sibling!

We praise and adore how much our fantastic, furry family members express their own unique personalities. We're amazed by their wide range of emotions and sincere loyalty towards us. We can't deny their genuine love and devotion they gift us with until they take their very last breath.

carnism:
the invisible belief system that conditions us to eat certain animals.

On the other hand, most of us have also been raised consuming other kinds of animals such as pigs, chickens, cows, and turkeys. After all, it was always considered "normal, natural, and necessary," which made it subconsciously justifiable. The misconception that we needed to eat meat and drink dairy to maintain a healthy, balanced diet is another reason why we acted against our values without fully realizing what we were doing. It was our carnistic defenses that suppressed our contradictory beliefs and blocked our natural-born empathy for animals.

This can be partially attributed to our constant exposure to crafty and persuasive messages we've aimlessly "downloaded" while growing up. Methodically, this devious program has been carefully designed to influence our young minds' attitudes and behaviors supportive of industrial livestock production, or "factory farming."

Major companies who own or influence large-scale agriculture on farms is known as **corporate farming**. These corporations are highly involved in the selling of agricultural products while also having leverage on agricultural education, research, and public policy through funding initiatives and lobbying efforts.

Gummy worms are made out of gelatin, which is made from the tissue, skin, and bones of pigs and cows.

Social Conditioning

Our society as a whole has grown up to be pet lovers, but not so much *animal lovers*. As a result, an emotional disconnection from certain animals is all too common.

Animals who are labeled as 'food' compared to 'pets' sadly live their shortened lives much differently. Ironically, it's been shown that large majorities of the human population would agree that all animals should be treated humanely and not made to suffer. Once you can make the connection between consuming animals with pain and suffering, you may begin to develop a heightened sense of compassion and empathy.

Pigs are someone, not something.
Pigs have been found to be mentally
and socially similar to dogs and chimpanzees.

Photo: @estherthewonderpig

Two domesticated animals:

Dogs: selected for traits promoting human companionship and work.

Pigs: selected for the ability to produce meat.

Growing up with an impressionable mind, it's only natural to process and internalize certain expectations and beliefs placed upon us. The roles of animals who are accepted as pets versus the roles of animals widely accepted as food enables people to avoid **cognitive dissonance**. This is defined by *Merriam-Webster* as a "psychological conflict resulting from incongruous beliefs and attitudes held simultaneously."

How can we respect and adore certain kinds of animals yet torture and devour other kinds? Learned programming throughout our early years and beyond can be stored in our biology, creating subconscious patterns that dictate our current and daily habits.

Re-aligning your personal perception of animals can help you make the *re-connection* between your feelings, beliefs, and actions towards such sentient beings. This definitely takes a bit self-awareness, self-reflection, and self-acceptance.

Section 3 - The Mass Production of Animals

Long gone are the sustainable family-run farms in which cows, pigs, and chickens roamed around freely on farm owners' lands. It was in the 1970s when pig farmers made their transition into factory farming. They followed the example of massive corporate operations that began hiring poultry farmers as "contract growers" to mass produce animal products for them in the 1930s and 40s.

These factory farms, sometimes referred to as **Concentrated Animal Feeding Operations (CAFOs)** are the locations where animals have sadly become units of production. Billions of animals are denied their natural habitats and experience a life of physical pain, mental torture, and social suffering.

General Consequences of CAFOs
- They produce a lot of pollutants - urine and feces run into waterways
- They're killing our planet - over 160 different types of gases are emitted
- They're breeding grounds for viruses, infections, contagious diseases - overcrowding of animals, the animals' compromised immune systems from stress, ammonia from decomposing waste burning their lungs, and deplorable living conditions threatens the emergence and spread of disease among themselves and onto humans
- The use of antibiotics to promote unnatural growth of animals contributes to the development of antibiotic-resistant pathogens in humans
- They cause major ethical harm to animals who feel mental and physical pain

Human Health Consequences of Factory Farming

Facts you should know:

- Animal products made for human consumption are the primary source of saturated fat in the standard American diet. Studies have shown that animal feeds used to promote unnatural growth of factory-farmed animals increase the saturated fat content of meat. Saturated fat has been clearly linked to heart disease and obesity.

- Cows in the dairy industry are typically injected with bioengineered growth hormones to produce more milk than their bodies normally would. The six growth hormones commonly used by the U.S. dairy industry have been shown to significantly increase the risk of breast, prostate, and colon cancer in beef consumers. Producers are not required to disclose the use of hormones on product labels.

- According to the FDA, more than 20 million pounds of medically important antibiotic drugs were sold for use on livestock farms in 2014 — about 80% of all antibiotics sold.[1] Each year in the U.S., at least 2.8 million people get an antibiotic-resistant infection according to the Centers for Disease Control and Prevention.[2]

rBGH or recombinant growth hormone: is just one lab-made growth hormone that's created to mimic the bovine growth hormone that cows naturally produce in their bodies. It's been shown to increase the level of another hormone called insulin-like growth factor (IGF-1) in the cow.

Higher levels of IGF-1 in human patients have been shown to encourage the growth of cancer cells and likely be a cause of breast cancer.[4]

- Poor sanitation and waste management on factory farms and the poor management of animal waste leads to the contamination of the food supply by bacteria such as E. Coli and salmonella. Each year, 48 million Americans become sick from food borne illness.[3]

- Certain diseases, such as H1N1 (swine flu) and the avian flu, are communicable from animals to humans. These zoonotic diseases have the potential to cause more pandemics. Some experts believe that the outbreak of H1N1 was likely caused by the overcrowding of pigs on factory farms and the storage of their waste in giant manure lagoons.

Factory Farms - breeding grounds for zoonotic diseases

Intensive animal farming, also known as factory farming, has become the norm with an estimated 99% of U.S. farm animals being raised in this system.

Data from the 2017 USDA Census of Agriculture reveals that 70.4% of cows, 98.3% of pigs, 99.8% of turkeys, 98.2% of chickens raised for eggs, and over 99.9% of chickens raised for meat are raised in factory farms.[5]

Infectious disease: a disease caused by bacteria, viruses, fungi, or parasites that can be transferred to humans.

Zoonotic disease (pl. zoonoses): an infectious animal disease that is naturally transmitted to human beings, either through the person's direct exposure to the animals, via air or water, or by consuming food made of the animals.

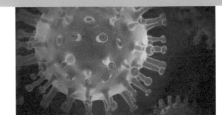

An epidemic is a disease that affects a large number of people within a community, population, or region.

A pandemic is an epidemic that's spread over multiple countries or continents.

Humankind is at risk

Animals can carry harmful germs including viruses, bacteria, parasites and fungi that can spread to people. Moreover, about 60% of all known infectious diseases in humans are zoonotic diseases, as are 75% of emerging ones according to a 2016 UN report.[6]

As history shows and in more recent times, global pandemics caused by zoonotic diseases continue to be a deadly threat to humans, our economy, and our livelihood.

Farm houses are horror houses

The industrialization of livestock farming has led to more opportunities for exposure to food borne pathogens. Factory farms are likened to incubators for the emergence of highly disease-causing strains.

In the US, the total number of broilers produced in 2019 was 9.18 billion. Source: USDA/NASS Poultry Production and Value 2019 Summary
Photo: @human.cruelties

> "Factory farming is a perfect-storm environment for infectious diseases."
>
> — Dr. Michael Greger, author of *Bird Flu: A Virus of Our Own*

The overcrowding of animals who are bred intensely can facilitate the spread of disease. Such animals are highly susceptible to infection due to immunosuppression from chronic stress, unsanitary conditions, and unnatural forced growth via injected hormones. Common transmission of zoonoses occurs through the animal shedding or when people are exposed to bodily fluids, blood, and secretions. Workers who slaughter the animals are clearly at greater risk.

In 2004, the Food and Agriculture Organization of the United Nations (FAO), The World Health Organization (WHO), and the World Organization for Animal Health (OIE, world leader in veterinary authority) came out with a report from a joint consultation on emerging zoonotic diseases. They found that, "anthropogenic (human-caused) factors such as agricultural expansion and intensification to meet the increasing demand for animal protein" are one of the major drivers of zoonotic disease emergence.[7]

Zoonotic spillover has increased in the last 50 years, mainly due to the environmental impact of agriculture that promotes deforestation, changing wildlife habitat, and the impacts of increased land use.[8]

zoonotic spillover:
the transmission of pathogens from nonhuman animals to us

Zoonotic diseases, which are sometimes linked to wet markets, are yet another clear realization that handling or coming into close contact with wildlife — along with their body parts and/or excretions like blood, spit and urine (hence, wet market) — can lead to an inevitable zoonotic spillover of pathogens they host, resulting in a deadly, worldwide outbreak.

It's fairly clear to see that protecting wildlife and their natural habitats, while respecting animals and their spaces, can reduce the transmission of zoonoses and its potentially detrimental effects on human lives.

Actionable Step Towards Going Vegan #2

Reflect back to your childhood and think of a couple ways that may have prompted you to include meat and dairy as part of your diet. Is there anything that stands out in particular? This can happen through various influences such as through our typical family upbringing, culture or tradition, or by the media.

For example, I remember the dairy industry's "Got Milk?" campaign. Admiring different kinds of athletes with their "milk mustaches" somehow convinced me that drinking milk would help me become a better athlete. Their use of celebrity ambassadors seemed to be pretty effective, too. I also *acquired the belief* that drinking dairy milk would help me develop strong bones, grow taller, and be able to date the prettiest girl in school.

Do you remember those "strategic" advertisements?

Seeing happy cows on cartons of milk and on cheese product labels may have also contributed to creating a disconnect regarding how cows truly feel on an actual machine producing dairy farm or inside of a dark, gory slaughterhouse. Whether meat, eggs, or dairy is sold as "farm raised" or "organic," the animals all end up being slaughtered inhumanely.

For me, growing up as half Filipino, it was traditional to eat lechon (roasted suckling pig) when attending parties and family potlucks. This was served at most special occasions and during the holiday seasons and festivals.

Can you think of other ways you were influenced to consume animal products? I'd love to hear your thoughts and personal experiences.

Contact us and share your story at goingvegan4goodness.com

Photo: @human.cruelties

Protecting the silenced

There is plenty of evidence-based research showing that individuals from a wide range of species do experience emotions. They can range from joy and happiness, to deep sadness, grief, and post-traumatic stress disorder. They can also feel empathy, jealousy and even resentment. Just like us, animals want to live in peace and safety without fear, pain or suffering.

Millions of people have already made the connection to the reality of what really goes on behind livestock production. As a true animal lover, your vegan journey may stem from your personal values and beliefs coming from your heart. Listening to what your heart is telling you can allow you to acknowledge what other animals may be feeling. This characteristic sense of moral intelligence can help you understand right from wrong while having the ability to act on that understanding.

sentient being:
one who has the ability to feel, perceive, or be conscious, or to experience subjectivity

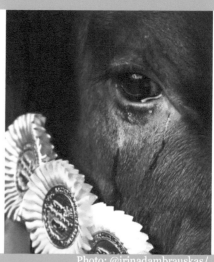

Photo: @irinadambrauskas/ @thesavemovement

Photo: @human.cruelties

A mindful process

With the massive progression of intensive factory farming and its detrimental effects on our personal health and our planet, now more than ever, it's critical to practice ***mindful eating.***

We can do this by asking ourselves at mealtimes - *who, what, where, why, and how* am I eating?

empathy:
the imaginative projection of one's own consciousness into another being; the ability to understand and share the feelings of another.

Section 4 - For Our Planet and Her Inhabitants

Forests all around the world are cleared for the purpose of livestock production. Sadly, entire populations of animals are killed, are becoming extinct, or are being displaced. It is estimated that 135 species become extinct *every single day*.

Dairy and meat products take up 83% of global farmland, yet provide just 18% of human calories and 37% of global protein.[1]

By 2050, consumption of meat and dairy products is expected to rise 76% and 64% respectively.[2] As a result of higher demand, this places an even greater burden on our planet's resources. Additionally, the biggest source of emissions from animal agriculture are cattle. In an average American diet, beef consumption creates 1,984 pounds of CO_2e (carbon dioxide equivalent) annually.[3] Replacing beef with plants would reduce that figure by 96 percent, lowering it to just 73 pounds of CO_2e.[4]

Animal agriculture is a major culprit of the current mass extinction of wildlife and is a leading cause of deforestation, biodiversity loss, and water pollution.

The Leopard, Asian Elephants, Hyacinth Macaw, and Mountain Gorillas are among the thousands of endangered rainforest animals.

What Is Deforestation?

Deforestation, which is also known as clearcutting, is simply the removal of a forest or standing trees for the purpose of using that land for something else. The cleared land is then made into farms, plantations, roads, housing, and other uses to further urbanization.

Two major reasons for deforestation:
1. Food production
2. Timber production

Deforestation has become a major cause of global climate change affecting each and every one of us. According to the Food And Agriculture Organization of the United Nations, if we keep up with the current rate that we are cutting down trees, we will destroy all the rainforests on earth within the next 100 years.[5]

Climate scientists attribute climate change to natural disasters and social issues including:

- Floods
- Drought
- Wildfires
- Cyclones
- Hurricanes
- Heat Waves
- Climate Immigrants
- Health & well-being of Indigenous Tribes

"A vegan diet is probably the single biggest way to reduce your impact on planet Earth, not just greenhouse gases, but global acidification, eutrophication, land use and water use."

— Joseph Poore, University of Oxford, Research author of *"Reducing food's environmental impacts through producers and consumers"*[6]

Why Are Trees So Important To Us?

A single tree produces enough oxygen for 3 people to breathe.

Trees also...
- stabilize the soil
- help reduce noise
- purify the air we breathe
- absorb nasty pollutants
- are good for our mental health
- give life to our world's wildlife
- cleanse the air by intercepting airborne particles
- remove air pollution by lowering air temperature
- are large carbon sinks - they hold more carbon than they release making them critical for our planet and our existence

The lungs of our planet

We absolutely need forests to survive. Trees provide us and other animals with fresh air. They absorb the carbon dioxide (CO_2) we breathe out and transform it into clean oxygen (O_2). They are the second largest carbon sink in the world. For this reason, we need to protect them as they are critical allies in the fight against climate change.

What we choose to buy and eat can make a world of a difference

If we eliminated meat and dairy production, farmland would be reduced by 75%, allowing our world's ecosystems to recover from deforestation and its harmful effects.[7] On top of that, we would still be able to produce enough food to feed all of humanity.

Effects of Meat Production on our Ocean Environment

Animal agriculture does not only affect our precious land resources. It is damaging our ocean's health and marine life, too. As a result of common modern day animal agriculture practices including concentrated animal feeding operations (CAFOs), **nutrient pollution** has become more wide-spread since the 1970s. This has led to an increase of anthropogenic (human-caused) *dead zones* in our oceans, streams, lakes, and ponds.

The primary source of eutrophication leading to dead zones from animal agriculture is improper disposal of manure.

Photo: A flooded CAFO taken by Jo-Anne McArthur @weanimalsmedia

eutrophication: when a body of water becomes overly enriched with minerals and nutrients. Nutrients feed algae, and then the algae grows and blocks sunlight. Plants underneath die without sunlight. Eventually, the algae dies, too. Bacteria then digests the dead plants, using up remaining oxygen, and giving off carbon dioxide.

Hypoxia (or oxygen depletion) from harmful algal blooms can destroy aquatic life in affected areas.

These nutrients, which are typically phosphate and nitrates, come from animal waste, fertilizers and sewage. They get washed by rain or irrigation into the water bodies through surface run-off. In addition, there is excess fertilizer run-off from the production of animal feeds such as corn and soy. It's because of all these issues that animal agriculture has become one of the leading causes of ocean dead zones.

These ocean dead zones are areas of large bodies of water that can no longer contain enough oxygen to sustain marine life. Ocean dead zones negatively impact coastal ecosystem functioning, predator-prey relationships, and can cause immobile organisms to die in such low-oxygen conditions.

Harmful algal blooms can have negative impacts on humans, marine and freshwater environments, and coastal economies.

Actionable Step Towards Going Vegan #3

Start becoming more conscious of the foodstuff and other products you purchase. Before buying anything, find out what it's made out of and how it was made. Being a conscious consumer and declining to buy anything that contains animal products or that promotes animal exploitation helps reduce the demand for animal-derived products and services.

Mother Nature depends on us

Meat production is known to be one of the largest contributors to global deforestation. The world's demand for beef, chicken, and pork is a leading cause of habitat loss, resource use, and greenhouse gas emissions.

In addition, large scale meat suppliers and producers have been linked with illegal deforestation using environmentally protected land for cattle ranching.

Just four commodities drive the majority of tropical deforestation:[8]

1.   **Beef** - the forest conversion that beef production generates is more than double what's generated by the production of soy, palm oil, and wood products combined.[9]
2.   **Soybeans** - primarily used to feed pork, poultry, and dairy cows, though significant amounts are also used to produce vegetable oil and bio-diesel.
3.   **Palm oil** - commonly used in processed foods and personal care products, as well as bio-fuels and vegetable oil.
4.   **Wood products** - pulp used to make paper, paper products and fabric, as well as timber used for construction and high end products, are linked to forest degradation.

Every single purchase we make is a show of support of the particular brand or company. The money we spend is a reflection of who and why we support the specific products or services, including the practices and morals of the company. Therefore, it's important to be an educated, conscious consumer so that with every dollar (or other currency) you spend, you're supporting something you truly believe in.

Section 5 - Social Impact

Human Freedom

Animal agriculture has a major impact on the lives of people all around the world. Thousands of factory farm workers, many of whom are undocumented immigrants, tend to work long hours under harsh and stressful conditions for minimum wage.

Workers in the meat and dairy industries are often exploited for their cheap and silent labor. Due to the fear of losing their jobs or being deported, they can feel powerless in requesting better pay or asking for safer working conditions.

Higher mental disorder levels and poorer vitality have been reported for animal and dairy farmers compared to non-farmers.[1]

Workers are also susceptible to injuries, contagious diseases, viruses, and infections. Working under such dangerous and unsanitary conditions is the norm and tends to be ignored.

The psychological effects may even be worse than physical injuries. Every day, employees are exposed to the sights and sounds of fear, misery, and brutal deaths of sentient beings. The daily routine of killing more than 40 animals/minute for extremely low pay may be a likely factor in the harmful symptoms of PTSD, anxiety, and other related mental health conditions commonly observed in slaughterhouse workers.

A Breath of Destructive Pollution

Factory farms are not regulated when it comes to pollution. As a result, factory farms are allowed to pollute local water and air supplies almost without restriction. The millions of tons of manure produced by farm animals in the United States alone contributes to polluting the air and local water supply, killing local wildlife and making nearby residents sick.

Food and Water Supply

If humans stopped using land and edible crops to feed animals bred and killed for meat and dairy, **we could potentially end world hunger**.

Raising animals for food (including land for grazing and growing feed crops) currently uses over one-third of the planet's landmass. If this space were used to grow edible plants, we could not only save the 70+ billion land animals killed each year for food, but we could also feed the 815 million humans who suffer from starvation.

Meat Wastes Water

The water footprint from animals comes mostly from the water required to grow the feed. To produce beef, 98% goes towards growing the feed, but the cow only drinks 1.1% of the water.[3]

"Today, half the world's agricultural land is used for livestock farming...which is far less efficient for feeding people— and worse for the environment— than producing grain, fruit, and vegetables for direct human consumption."

— U.N. Officials

Almost half of all the water used in the United States goes towards raising animals for food. This includes irrigating the crops that are grown for farmed animals to eat, providing the billions of animals water to drink each year, and other uses while transporting and slaughtering animals.

2,400 gallons of water is required to produce 1 lb. of beef
25 gallons of water is required to grow 1 lb. of wheat[2]

Section 6 - Human Health & Wellness

More and more studies are showing that **animal-based foods are linked to human health issues**. The box below contains a list revealing the Top 10 health concerns linked to animal food consumption.[1]

1. Heart Disease
2. Cancer
3. Stroke
4. Diabetes
5. Obesity
6. Harmful Cholesterol
7. Acne
8. Erectile Dysfunction
9. Alzheimer's Disease
10. Shorter Lifespan

Cardiovascular diseases are the number one cause of death globally.[5]

The most important behavioral risk factors of heart disease and stroke include an unhealthy diet, physical inactivity, tobacco use, and harmful use of alcohol.

Standard American Diet (SAD)

The typical standard American diet is high in calories, saturated fat, sodium, and added sugars. It also lacks enough fruits, vegetables, whole grains, calcium, and fiber. This type of diet contributes to some of the leading causes of death and increases the risk of various diseases,[2] including:

- heart disease
- diabetes
- obesity
- stroke
- high blood pressure
- osteoporosis[3], and
- cancers, including cervical, colon, gallbladder, kidney, liver, ovarian, uterine, and postmenopausal breast cancers; leukemia; and esophageal cancer (after researchers took smoking into account).[4]

Processed Meat - A Group I Carcinogen

A carcinogen is something that causes cancer in humans. Other common examples of carcinogens include tobacco, arsenic, and pesticides.

In 2015, the World Health Organization (WHO) International Agency for Research on Cancer (IARC) announced that processed meat was classified as ***carcinogenic to humans (Group 1)***, based on sufficient evidence that the consumption of processed meat causes colorectal cancer.

They also stated that the consumption of red meat is ***probably carcinogenic to humans (Group 2A)***, based on limited evidence that the consumption of red meat causes cancer in humans and strong mechanistic evidence supporting a carcinogenic effect.

Bacon, hot dogs, and salami are all among the same group as tobacco, according to the IARC's Carcinogenic Classification.

Processed meat
–meat that has been transformed through salting, curing, fermentation, smoking, or other processes to enhance flavor or improve preservation.

Red meat
–unprocessed mammalian muscle meat such as beef, veal, pork, lamb, mutton, horse, and goat.

According to Marji McCullough, Ph.D., a nutritional epidemiologist with the American Cancer Society, "the association between consumption of red and processed meats and cancer, particularly colorectal cancer, is very consistent."

Eating meat exposes humans to carcinogens, compromises blood flow, and increases oxidative stress and inflammation, which are also linked to premature aging.

The (Detrimental) Power of Food

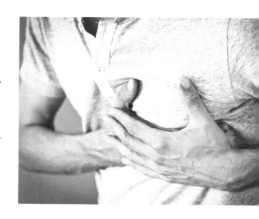

Saturated fat is a main dietary culprit in the buildup of plaque in the arteries. Over a prolonged period of time, the plaque builds up and hardens in the arteries, causing narrowing of the blood vessels' walls. This buildup of plaque (atherosclerosis) can lead to our world's number one killer, **heart disease.**

It can also lead to stroke, cancer, and diabetes. These preventable chronic diseases are the leading causes of death and disability in America. They also happen to be the leading driver of health care costs.

A primary source of saturated fat is animal products.

Examples of food high in saturated fat include:

Butter
High-fat cheese
Whole milk and cream
Ice cream (made from dairy)
High-fat cuts of meat (marbled meat)
Processed meats like sausages and bologna
Palm and coconut oils, which are often added to packaged and prepared foods, such as cookies, doughnuts, and even 'healthy' energy bars

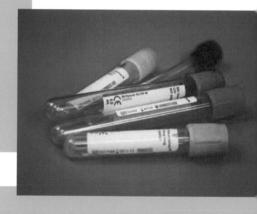

According to the Centers for Disease Control and Prevention (CDC), six in ten Americans live with at least one chronic disease.[6]

The CDC also states that most chronic diseases can be prevented by eating well, being physically active, avoiding tobacco and excessive drinking, and getting regular health screenings.

The number of people diagnosed with diabetes in 2019 was 463 million.

The projected number of people with diabetes is expected to reach 700 million by 2045.[7]

If we know that there are ways for us to avoid getting these diseases, we need to ask ourselves — what else can we do about it?

Section 7 - What Is A Vegan Diet?

A "vegan diet" contains only plants (such as vegetables, grains, nuts and fruits) and foods made from plants.

Vegans don't eat foods that come from animals, including dairy products and eggs; however, going on a "vegan diet" doesn't necessarily mean you're eating healthier. Dietary quality is not just about leaving animal products off your plate.

100% plant-based/vegan burger

A *healthy vegan diet* really comes down to how much processed or refined plant fragments (sugars, oils, refined flours) you choose to eat.

With good planning and an understanding of what makes up a healthy, balanced vegan or plant-based diet, you can certainly get all the nutrients your body needs.

Incorporating a vegan diet and lifestyle will look and feel different for everyone. The foods and dishes shared in this book are meant to introduce just some of the varieties of plant-based food sources while showing you how versatile they can be for cooking.

Please consult with your physician when considering a vegan diet, especially if you're taking any kind of medication or are pregnant or breastfeeding.

Types of Foods Vegans Eat

Whole Grains (4-6+ servings per day)

Whole grains are grains that have not had the outer bran layer or the "germ" part removed. They are more nutritious than refined grains because the refining process removes the healthiest nutrients. This makes them richer in vitamins, minerals and fiber, which are essential for our bodies.

Examples are brown rice, rolled oats, corn, quinoa, and barley. Products made from whole meal flour, such as pasta, bread, and crackers are also in this group. If choosing breakfast cereals, look for varieties that are 100% whole grain.

A serving is 1 slice of bread, 1/2 cup of cooked grain, or 1 ounce of ready-to-eat cereal. This group is fairly flexible with regard to servings per day. Vary your intake based on your individual energy needs.

Vegetables (4+ servings per day)

Vegetables are low in fat but rich in essential nutrients. The most important vegetables to eat every day are green, leafy vegetables. They are particularly rich in nutrients and other health-enhancing components. Kale, spinach, collard greens, and arugula are good healthy examples.

It is also important to eat red/orange/yellow vegetables as these are rich in pro-vitamin A and other health-enhancing antioxidants. Examples include carrots, pumpkin, yellow squash, sweet potato, sweet corn, red and yellow capsicum and tomatoes.

No single vegetable or fruit provides all of the nutrients you need to be healthy, so be sure to eat plenty every day.

A vegetable serving is 1/2 cup cooked, 1 cup raw, or 1/2 cup of juice.

Evidence suggests that a whole food plant-based diet can not only prevent, but treat, coronary artery disease (CAD), which is the leading cause of death in the United States in both men and women.[1]

Fruit (2+ servings per day)

It's good to eat a wide variety of fruits. Try to choose some that are rich in vitamin C such as mango, pineapple, berries, and kiwifruit. Fresh, whole fruit is the best choice, as processing fruit destroys valuable nutrients.

Examples include apples, bananas, mangoes, blueberries, gooseberries, strawberries, figs, and Goji berries.

A fruit serving size is 1 medium piece, 1 cup sliced, 1/4 cup dried, or 1/2 cup of juice.

Legumes, Nuts, Seeds (4+ servings per day)

Legumes is a general term used to describe the seeds of plants from the legume family, which includes beans, peas, lentils, and peanuts. This group also includes soy products such as tofu, tempeh, and textured vegetable protein (TVP).

Nuts and seeds can be eaten whole or ground, or in paste form such as peanut butter and tahini (sesame paste). These nutrient-dense foods are packed with protein, fiber, minerals, B vitamins, protective antioxidants, and essential fatty acids.

Sample serving sizes include: 1/2 cup of cooked beans, 4 ounces of tofu or tempeh, 1 cup of soy milk, 1 ounce of nuts or seeds, or 2 tablespoons of nut or seed butter.

Beans are the seeds of legumes.

Examples include peas, lentils, soybeans, mung beans, and chickpeas.

Nuts are the seeds of trees. Examples include walnuts, hazelnuts, Brazil nuts, and pecans.

A seed is a small embryonic plant enclosed in a covering called the seed coat, usually with some stored food. Examples of seeds include sesame, flax, poppy seeds, chia, and sunflower.

Plant Milks

Plant milks are vegan, and many contain a great amount of nutritional value. Compared to dairy, they're also much better options for lowering your environmental impact.

Ditching dairy for plant-based milks is one major way to support animal welfare while decreasing your carbon footprint.

What's a plant milk?

Plant-based milks are milks made from grains, beans, seeds, and nuts.

There's an alternative for everyone. Whether you are looking for milk that is lactose-free, nut-free, gluten-free, or low-fat, you are good to go! Best of all, you're not paying for someone to inflict pain and suffering against any kind of dairy animal and their babies.

Soy milk is the only plant-based option that contains the same amount of protein as cow's milk. It contains omega-3 fatty acids, fiber, manganese, and magnesium, making it a popular plant-based milk alternative.

Made from soybeans or soy flour, it contains calcium, iron, and Riboflavin (B2). Soy is not linked to an increased risk of breast cancer (as once believed). Drinking soy milk may actually help protect against it, according a February 2020 study published in the *International Journal of Epidemiology*.[2]

Plant-based milks are:

• The compassionate choice
No animals are harmed, forcefully impregnated, or separated from their babies

• Better for our environment
There's a significant decrease in greenhouse gas emissions and water usage compared to traditional dairy

• Lactose-free
Around 70% of adults worldwide have some degree of lactose intolerance

• Much healthier
Unlike dairy milk, plant milks do not contain carcinogenic proteins, antibiotics, and hormones

It takes 976 gallons of water to produce just 1 gallon of dairy milk.

Plants have protein!
Soy and hemp milks are great choices for getting plant protein in your diet. Both soy and hemp are complete proteins providing all nine essential amino acids.

Plant-based milks do not contain lactose or cholesterol and many brands are manufacturing them with fortified vitamins A and D, calcium, and vitamin B12. They tend to have fewer calories due to less fat (except for coconut-based milk), and have greater water content, which can help improve your hydration.

Remember to check the labels of each brand. Be aware of brands that add high amounts of sugar and salt.

You make a difference each and every time you choose to drink plant-based milk (and eat delicious non-dairy ice cream) over cow's milk. You're helping to prevent mothers and babies from being subjected to the misery of separation and unnecessarily harsh forms of emotional abuse.

Millions of people have already ditched cow's milk for health reasons or intolerance to dairy. Ethical concerns about animal abuse in modern dairy farming practices are another good reason to choose plant-milks. Many have also made the switch simply for taste and preference.

Oat milk. It does a body, mind, and planet better.™

For those of you who can relate to mullets, leg warmers, and shoulder pad blazers of the 80s, you'll recognize what this modernized, more accurate catchphrase is all about. Contrary to the dairy milk ad campaigns of old, which flooded TV screens all throughout the US, oat milk truly does *do* a body good.

"Milk. It does a body good."

On April 27, 1983, the California Milk Producers Advisory Board filed a trademark to use this advertising slogan in their marketing campaigns. The campaign positioned milk as necessary for strong bones and to prevent osteoporosis.

If you experience digestive symptoms such as bloating, diarrhea, abdominal pain, or gas after drinking milk, then odds are you have lactose intolerance. Simply put, baby calves are meant to drink their mother's milk — just like human babies are meant to drink their own mother's milk.

Human consumption of cow's milk and the link to causing health problems such as ear infections, allergies, cancer, and diabetes[3] may be enough reason to realize that milk truly isn't good for any human's body.

What's so good about oats?

Oats are a super nutritious food packed with key vitamins, minerals, and antioxidants. Plus, they're high in soluble fiber and protein compared to other grains. A study published in *The Journals of Gerontology* found that people who consumed more dietary fiber experienced a lower risk of age-related diseases and disability, including cognitive problems.[4] Another study that used research data from the National Health and Nutrition Examination Survey found that fiber may be beneficial to depression.[5]

And by ditching dairy, you'll help provide what's not only better, but essential for our planet and her inhabitants. That's because grazing dairy cows negatively contribute to deforestation and greenhouse gas emissions, which affects every living being on earth.

Thus, you can count on oat milk over dairy milk to help boost your physical and mental health benefits while protecting our precious planet.

How is oat milk better?

It's lactose-free.

It contains zero cholesterol and zero saturated fat.

The fiber in oats can help stabilize your blood sugar.[6]

It provides about 3 grams of protein and 2 grams of fiber per cup.

Oats are naturally gluten-free, making it a good, safe choice for those with gluten sensitivities or celiac disease.

Oats naturally contain vitamins and minerals including thiamin, folate, magnesium, manganese, zinc, and copper.

Most commercial oat milk brands are also fortified with vitamins A, D, B12 and B2, calcium, potassium, and iron.

Oat milk's prebiotic fiber helps to balance out your gut microbiome, which scientists say can benefit your mental health.

Consuming the fiber in oats has been linked to controlling mood swings and irritability.[7]

Growing oats has a relatively low-impact on the environment requiring a lesser amount of water and land use compared to dairy and other plant milk alternatives.

You'll contribute to less greenhouse gas emissions and support our earth's sustainability when choosing a glass of oat milk over dairy milk.

Remember to be mindful that each brand's nutritional content will vary depending on any added sweeteners or other flavors.

When purchasing oat milk, be sure to choose a brand that's certified organic or states on the label that their oats are glyphosate-free, carrageenan-free, phosphate-free and gluten free.

Next time you go to the grocery store, be sure to grab a carton of plant-based milk. Check the label and make sure it's fortified with vitamin B12, vitamins A and D and calcium.

Better yet, try making your own nut or seed milk!

How to make your own nut or seed milk:

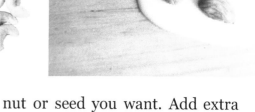

You can use the instructions below for any type of nut or seed you want. Add extra flavors and sweeten it up with other ingredients like a date, a splash of vanilla, some cinnamon, or a dash of Himalayan salt.

Instructions:

1. Soak nuts or seeds overnight in filtered water in a mason jar with the lid on in the fridge. Be sure they're covered by at least 2 inches of water.

2. Drain and rinse the nuts or seeds the next morning and put them in a blender. A Vitamix or other powerful blender works best.

3. Add fresh filtered water in a 4:1 ratio (for example, 4 cups of water and 1 cup of nuts or seeds). Add any additional ingredients you'd like, such as a pinch of cinnamon, sweetener, or vanilla.

4. Blend well.

Depending on the nuts or seeds you use, you may need to strain your milk through a nut milk bag. Place it over a large pitcher or other container and squeeze the liquid out.

Homemade nut milk may last in the fridge for up to 3 to 4 days.
I recommend making small batches and regularly changing up the nuts and seeds you use. Switching them up will allow you to taste different kinds of plant milks and can also help determine which is easiest for you to make. Choosing a variety of nuts and seeds that are in season is also a great way to maintain a healthy, nutritious, eco-conscious way of eating.

Section 8 - Vitamins, Essential Fatty Acids, Minerals

The only vitamins that are not readily obtainable from unprocessed plant foods are vitamins D and B12. It is important for anyone eating a vegan diet to know where to get them from.

Vitamin D - otherwise known as the "sunshine vitamin," is also a hormone; our skin manufactures it from the ultraviolet rays of the sun. It plays an important role in bone health and supports normal neuromuscular and immune function. Good vitamin D status is linked to a lowered risk of osteoporosis, certain cancers, and other chronic diseases.

It is found almost exclusively in animal products including fatty fish, like tuna, mackerel, and salmon. It's also prevalent in beef liver, egg yolk, and cheese.

The best sources of vitamin D for vegans are:

Fortified plant milks including soy, almond, and rice
Fortified cereals
Fortified orange juice
Mushrooms (UV light exposed mushrooms)
Good old-fashioned sunshine

It's important to be mindful about vitamin D. The latest research suggests that even getting 100% of the current Recommended Dietary Allowance (RDA) for vitamin D may be insufficient for many people. To ensure adequate vitamin D intake, consider taking 1000-4000 International Units (IU) per day, depending upon your age and other individual needs.

Getting approximately 10-30 minutes of daily mild sun exposure, without sunscreen, is recommended. During winter or for those living in less sunny areas, vegan vitamin D supplements are also recommended.

Vitamin B12 - is naturally found in animal products, including fish, meat, poultry, eggs, and milk products. It's a vital nutrient that's required for red blood cell formation, cell metabolism, nerve function, and DNA synthesis.

B12 is produced by bacteria and is found in soil and waterways, but is not normally found in common plant foods. Because plants vary widely in their levels of this bacteria (and we tend to thoroughly clean our fruits and vegetables), you cannot rely on plant foods to meet your B12 needs. Don't worry, because you can still get your vitamin B12 by consuming dietary supplements or fortified foods.

Finding vegan sources of vitamin B12:

Look for brands that manufacture products fortified with vitamin B12. Carefully read food labels that will display this information. Common kinds of food that are typically fortified with vitamin B12 include:
• Bread and ready-to-eat cereals
• Almond milk, coconut milk, original soy milk
• Nutritional yeast (aka "nooch") is a fungus that is a vital ingredient in bread, beer, and a variety of other foods. It's often fortified with vitamin B12 and is also a complete protein providing all 9 essential amino acids. This excellent source of dietary fiber is sold as flakes, granules, or powder and can be found in the spice section or bulk bins of health food stores.

Dr. Thomas Campbell, author of *The China Study Solution: The Simple Way To Lose Weight And Reverse Illness, Using A Whole-Food, Plant-Based Diet,* recommends just enough supplementation to avoid clinical deficiency. He states that most people should supplement with a large enough dose that puts them in the range of "normal" lab test results. Anyone who eliminates, or even limits, animal-food consumption needs to take vitamin B12 supplements, particularly if you're breastfeeding or are pregnant.

A sublingual, spray, or liquid form of methyl cobalamin, which is a naturally occurring form of vitamin B12, is my personal choice. It's best to consult with your physician to determine what's most suitable for you and your personal needs.

Nutritional yeast, a vegan, Parmesan flavor-like cheese alternative, is commonly fortified with vitamin B12.

Actionable Step Towards Going Vegan #6

Since vegans (and non-vegans) may be prone to vitamin B12 deficiency, it's important for you to purchase a vitamin B12 dietary supplement. This is something that you don't want to take lightly due to the potential health issues.

When you don't eat animal products, you really only have two options in getting B12. You can either eat foods that have been fortified with vitamin B12, or you can take a vitamin B12 dietary supplement. Yup, that's it.

Vitamin B12, or cobalamin, is naturally found in animal foods or bacteria. Animals obtain vitamin B12 by eating foods that are covered in bacteria or from the bacteria that already line their own guts. As a human being, we have trillions of bacteria cells in our guts, but only in the large colon. Unfortunately, we are not able to absorb the vitamin B12 produced in the colon because it is only absorbed in the small intestine (which is upstream from the colon).

Deficiency may cause anemia, nerve damage, neurocognitive changes, and over time, paralysis. Thus, it's highly advisable for you to take a vitamin B12 dietary supplement.

Where can you buy vitamin B12?
You can purchase vegan B12 supplements online or at your local health food store. They come in the form of tablets, sublingual, sprays, or as a liquid.

Check the brand label's ingredients and description to ensure that they're vegan. Follow the instructions on how much of it to take and you'll be good to go.

Omega-3 - Vegans also require a good ratio of essential fatty acids (EFAs). Our body cannot produce EFAs on its own; therefore, we need to consume them as part of our diet.

Omega-3, also known as alpha linolenic acid (ALA), is normally consumed by eating fish and eggs; however, you can obtain EFAs from different food sources and/or from taking vegan ALA supplements.

One tablespoon of ground flaxseed contains about 1.8 grams of plant Omega-3s.

The best vegan sources of Omega-3 (ALA):

- flax seeds
- chia seeds
- walnuts
- hemp seeds
- edamame
- kidney beans
- soybean oil

The other type of Omega-3 fatty acid (EPA and DHA) can be obtained from algae, which is where fish get it from. Vegan algal supplements of EPA and DHA are also readily available at health food stores. Be sure to read product labels carefully.

The best vegan sources of Omega-3 (EPA and DHA):

- seaweed
- nori
- spirulina
- chlorella

Balancing Omega-3 and Omega-6 (typically found in processed food, tofu, nuts, and seeds) is important in preventing inflammation in the body. Including all three main types of Omega-3 (ALA, EPA, DHA) is also important in maintaining a balanced ratio of Omega-3 and Omega-6. To ensure you're getting the right amount, it's a good idea to speak with your physician, especially if you're pregnant.

Minerals

Just like vitamins, minerals are what's known as **essential nutrients**. This simply means that our body either cannot make these compounds or can't make enough of them. So then, where in the world can we get these essential nutrients from?

We can get them from colorful food, of course!

One easy way to know that you're getting a good amount of essential nutrients is to "eat the rainbow." Different colors of food represent specific nutrients. Basically, eating a variety of them makes it easy to know that you're (likely) getting a solid, well-balanced diet. For example, yellow and orange fruits and vegetables such as citrus fruits and gourds are abundant in vitamins C and A and potassium. Green fruits and veggies including kale, spinach, asparagus, and avocados are high in vitamins B, E, and K and iron, magnesium, and calcium. Purple produce like eggplant, red cabbage, and grapes are high in vitamins C and K and folate.

Rainbow salad by
Bayatakan Farm Experience;
Siargao, Philippines

Minerals are necessary for 3 main reasons:
1. building strong bones and teeth
2. controlling body fluids inside and outside cells
3. turning the food you eat into energy

Becoming more conscious about which minerals you need as part of your diet is an important part of living a healthy, vegan lifestyle.

Eat a rainbow everyday!

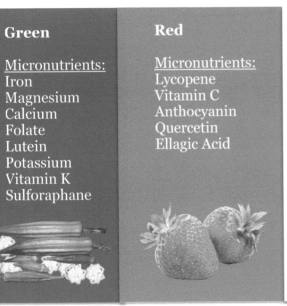

Green	Red	White/ Colorless	Blue/Purple	Orange
Micronutrients:	Micronutrients:	Micronutrients:	Micronutrients:	Micronutrients:
Iron	Lycopene	Flavanoids	Folate	Vitamin A
Magnesium	Vitamin C	Vitamin C	Vitamin C	Vitamin C
Calcium	Anthocyanin	Allium	Potassium	Beta Carotene
Folate	Quercetin	Sulforaphane		Alpha Carotene
Lutein	Ellagic Acid			Potassium
Potassium				
Vitamin K				
Sulforaphane				

Iron (Fe) - is part of hemoglobin in red blood cells and myoglobin in muscle cells. Iron helps to carry oxygen from the lungs to working cells throughout the body. Heme iron is predominantly found in meat (especially red meat). It is much better absorbed in the body than non-heme iron from plant foods.

Vegans can get all the iron we need from a vegan diet because there are lots of plant foods containing good amounts of this mineral. Cinnamon spice and oatmeal are two of my favorite sources. It's also important to avoid consuming too much iron, as it may cause some health issues.

It's beneficial to know that eating foods with vitamin C increases iron absorption, so be sure to eat plenty of food rich in this. Good sources of vitamin C include broccoli, cabbage, kiwifruit, oranges, strawberries, pineapple, and grapefruit.

Recommended Dietary Allowance	
Girls/Boys 4-8 yrs	10 mg/day
Girls/Boys 9-13 yrs	8 mg/day
Women 19-50 yrs	18 mg/day
Women 50+ yrs	8 mg/day
Men	8 mg/day

Source: National Center for Biotechnology Information, U.S. National Library of Medicine

Some Vegan Sources of Iron

Legumes: lentils, soybeans, tofu, tempeh, lima beans, black beans, chickpeas

Grains: quinoa, fortified cereals, brown rice, oatmeal

Nuts and Seeds: pumpkin, pine, pistachio, sunflower seeds, cashews, unhulled sesame, coconut

Vegetables: spinach, Swiss chard, collard greens, potato (baked with skin on), ginger root

Other: blackstrap molasses, cinnamon spice, prune juice

Calcium (Ca) - is a mineral that is necessary for life. We need it to build our bones and keep them healthy. Calcium also enables our blood to clot, our muscles to contract, and our heart to beat. About 99% of the calcium in our bodies is in our bones and teeth.

Non-vegans get most of their calcium from dairy products like milk, cheese, and yogurt. Vegans can get plenty of it from a variety of plant-based sources.

To absorb calcium in our intestines, our body also needs vitamin D. Remember, you can get vitamin D from fortified foods and from sufficient sun exposure, but if you're living in an area that doesn't get sufficient sunlight, especially during the winter time, consider taking vitamin D supplements. This will help boost calcium absorption.

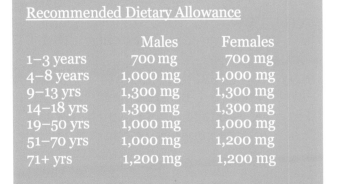

Recommended Dietary Allowance		
	Males	Females
1–3 years	700 mg	700 mg
4–8 years	1,000 mg	1,000 mg
9–13 yrs	1,300 mg	1,300 mg
14–18 yrs	1,300 mg	1,300 mg
19–50 yrs	1,000 mg	1,000 mg
51–70 yrs	1,000 mg	1,200 mg
71+ yrs	1,200 mg	1,200 mg

Source: National Institutes of Health Office of Dietary Supplements- US Department of Health and Human Services

Some Vegan Sources of Calcium

Legumes: pulses (edible seed that grows in a pod) including beans, lentils, chickpeas, and split peas

Grains: fortified oats and cereals

Nuts and Seeds: almonds, chia seeds, sesame seeds, and tahini

Vegetables: green, leafy vegetables such as broccoli, kale, cabbage, and bok choy

Fruits: oranges, okra, dried fruit such as raisins, prunes, figs, sweet cherries, and apricots

Iodine (I) - is an essential mineral used by the thyroid gland to make thyroid hormones that control many functions in the body, including growth and development. Because our body does not produce iodine on its own, it needs to be supplied in our diet.

Recommended Dietary Allowance	
Adults and adolescents	150 mcg/day
Pregnant and lactating women	250 mcg/day
Children aged 6-12 years	120 mcg/day
Infants to 6 years	90 mcg/day

Source: The World Health Organization

The major sources of iodine in the standard American diet include dairy products and seafood. Vegans are more prone to iodine deficiency because vegan sources of iodine are less abundant compared to animal sources of iodine.

Fruits and vegetables are not a reliable source of iodine. They cannot be counted on due to the variation in iodine content of soil. You can get some iodine from fruits and vegetables, but it's likely not enough to meet the daily requirements. Deficiency and toxicity are both possible, so please be sure that excess amounts are not taken either. Iodized salt is a reliable way to ensure adequate intake of iodine on a vegan diet. If you need to limit your salt intake, or are otherwise concerned about your intake of iodine, it's best to speak to a Registered Dietitian. Please consult with your physician if you're considering iodine supplements, which are another good source.

Some Vegan Sources of Iodine

Legumes: lima beans

Grains: fortified bread

Vegetables: seaweed varieties including kombu kelp, wakame and nori; organic potatoes with skin, watercress, and kale

Fruits: prunes, strawberries, green beans, zucchini

Other: iodized salt, iodine supplements

Zinc (Zn) - is an essential trace element that is necessary for our body's immune system to work properly. It also plays a role in cell growth, wound healing, and in breaking down carbohydrates.

Zinc is mainly found in animal protein sources, such as beef, pork and lamb. It is also more easily absorbed and used from animal protein sources. Thus, it's important to be mindful of where to get enough zinc.

Recommended Dietary Allowance	
Children 1–3 years	3 mg
Children 4–8 years	5 mg
Children 9–13 years	8 mg
Teens 14–18 years (boys)	11 mg
Teens 14–18 years (girls)	9 mg
Adults (men)	11 mg
Adults (women)	8 mg
Pregnant women	11 mg
Breastfeeding women	12 mg

Source: National Institutes of Health Office of Dietary Supplements - US Department of Health and Human Services

Some Vegan Sources of Zinc

Legumes: beans, chickpeas, lentils, tofu

Grains: oats, wheat germ, whole meal bread, quinoa

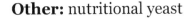

Nuts and Seeds: pumpkin seeds, sunflower seeds, walnuts, cashews, almonds, pecans, chia seeds, and hemp seeds

Vegetables: shiitake mushrooms, spinach, broccoli, kale, asparagus

Fruits: avocados, blackberries, pomegranates, raspberries, guavas, cantaloupes, apricots, peaches, kiwifruit, and blueberries

Other: nutritional yeast

Section 9 - Plant Protein

Whole Plant Foods Contain All Essential Nutrients (except B12)

In theory, vitamin and mineral supplements may not be necessary if your caloric intake is adequate and you include a variety of whole, plant-based foods. Individual vitamin and mineral needs do vary with age, gender, activity level, season, and climate. It's essential to develop greater awareness of your body's needs to live an optimal life.

Plant Protein

In addition to providing the building blocks for healthy muscles and tissues, plant protein can also be beneficial for weight loss. Plant-based proteins are generally lower in calories and fat than animal proteins and higher in fiber and essential nutrients.

Swapping out animal proteins for plant proteins can help you reduce your caloric intake while trimming off some unhealthy weight. Eating a variety of plant proteins is a good way to get all of the essential amino acids. It can be the healthiest way to get all of the vitamins, minerals, and other nutrients you need, too.

"I always say that eating a plant-based diet is the secret weapon of enhanced athletic performance."

— Rich Roll, vegan ultra-endurance athlete and author of *Finding Ultra*

Many experts believe that a well-planned vegan or plant-based diet can provide all the nutrients and essential amino acids that an individual needs to maintain a healthy, balanced lifestyle.

There is one question that every vegan gets asked, and that is...

"So...where do you get your protein from?"

Below are a few of many nutrient dense plant-based protein
sources and some examples of dishes you can consider making.
You can also add your own ideas in the space provided.

Plant Protein   Example Dishes/Uses

Adzuki Beans
1 cup
17.32 grams

- Chinese stir-fry with adzuki beans and Shiitake
- Pumpkin adzuki bean curry
- Anko sweet red bean paste

My veganized dish ideas:_____

_____

_____

Almonds
1/4 cup
7.56 grams

- Almond rosemary lemon crusted tofu
- Creamy vegan almond cheese
- Coconut almond truffles

My veganized dish ideas: _____

_____

_____

Amaranth
1 cup
9.35 grams

- Cauliflower schnitzel with puffed amaranth crust
- Protein power lentils and amaranth patties
- Popped amaranth peanut butter cups

My veganized dish ideas: _____

_____

_____

Plant Protein   Example Dishes/Uses

Black Beans
1 cup
15.24 grams

- Creamy black bean avocado dip
- Black bean tacos/burritos
- Spicy black bean burger

My veganized dish ideas: _____

_____

_____

_____

Black-eyed peas
1/2 cup
13.5 grams

- Chipotle black-eyed pea hummus
- Rosemary black-eyed pea soup with kale
- Southern style black-eyed pea salad

My veganized dish ideas: _____

_____

_____

_____

Chia Seeds
2 tablespoons
4.69 grams

- Sautéed zucchini with toasted chia seeds
- Raspberry banana chia seed smoothie
- Healthy vegan chia waffles

My veganized dish ideas: _____

_____

_____

_____

Plant Protein   **Example Dishes/Uses**

Cannellini Beans
1 cup
17.42 grams

- Garlic and white bean mashed potatoes
- Quinoa and white bean risotto
- Gooey chocolate chip pumpkin blondies

My veganized dish ideas: _____

_____

_____

_____

Edamame
1 cup
18.46 grams

- Spicy tofu and edamame stir fry
- Asian noodles with edamame
- Edamame pesto pasta

My veganized dish ideas: _____

_____

_____

_____

Flax Seeds
1 tablespoon
7.88 grams

- Flax seed meal muffins
- Mexican vegan meatloaf
- Cauliflower crust pizza

My veganized dish ideas: _____

_____

_____

_____

Plant Protein   Example Dishes/Uses

Garbanzo Beans
1 cup
14.53 grams

- Veggie tikka wraps with coconut chutney
- Berbere chickpea pizza with tahini sauce
- Mango curry chickpeas

My veganized dish ideas: _____

_____

_____

_____

Hazelnuts
1/2 cup
10 grams

- Hazelnut and chocolate bliss balls
- Blueberry hazelnut crumble bars
- Easy vegan Nutella

My veganized dish ideas: _____

_____

_____

_____

Hemp Seeds
1 tablespoon
9.47 grams

- Hemp falafel with sunflower seed dip
- Carrot cake energy bites with hemp
- Wild garlic and beet salad with hemp dressing

My veganized dish ideas: _____

_____

_____

_____

Plant Protein   Example Dishes/Uses

Lentils
1 cup
17.83 grams

- Butternut squash lentil soup
- Tuscan artichoke lentil stew
- Baked sweet potato with Moroccan lentils

My veganized dish ideas: _____

_____

_____

Oat Bran
1 cup
7.03 grams

- Almond joy oat bran granola bars
- Oatmeal breakfast cookies
- Blueberry oat bran muffins

My veganized dish ideas: _____

_____

_____

Pinto Beans
1 cup
15.41 grams

- Smoky pinto bean-beet burgers
- Pueblo corn pie casserole
- Cuban red beans and rice

My veganized dish ideas: _____

_____

_____

Studies have found that eating a plant-based diet can help manage type 2 diabetes. People who followed a plant-based diet showed greater improvements in blood sugar and cholesterol levels, body weight, and mental health compared with people who did not follow plant-based diets.[1]

Plant Protein   Example Dishes/Uses

Quinoa
1 cup
8.14 grams

- Buckwheat and quinoa pancakes
- Quinoa corn and avocado salad
- Quinoa with acorn squash and pomegranate

My veganized dish ideas: _____

_____

_____

_____

Sesame Seeds
1/4 cup
6.38 grams

- Savory sesame tofu bites
- Spinach salad with sesame dressing
- Sesame and coriander crusted grilled eggplant

My veganized dish ideas: _____

_____

_____

_____

Spirulina
1 tablespoon
4.02 grams

- Superfood banana bread
- Raw chocolate mint pie
- Matcha protein bars

My veganized dish ideas: _____

_____

_____

_____

Plant Protein   Example Dishes/Uses

Split Peas
1 cup
16.35 grams

- Cajun split pea and sweet potato stew
- Lebanese green split pea soup
- Indian yellow split pea dal

My veganized dish ideas: _____

_____

_____

_____

Sunflower Seeds
1/4 cup
7.27 grams

- Raw seed crisps
- Broccoli salad with raisins and sunflower seeds
- Cold soba noodle salad with raw veggie noodles and spicy sunflower seed sauce

My veganized dish ideas: _____

_____

_____

_____

Tempeh
1 cup
33.7 grams

- Veggie and tempeh Sloppy Joe's
- Korean BBQ tempeh wraps
- Tempeh Bolognese

My veganized dish ideas: _____

_____

_____

_____

Plant Protein   **Example Dishes/Uses**

Tofu
1 cup
16 grams

- Vegan battered tofu Mexican tortas
- Vegan Nashville hot tofu nuggets
- Teriyaki grilled tofu kabobs

My veganized dish ideas: _____

_____

_____

_____

Walnuts
1/4 cup
7.52 grams

- California walnut "chorizo" crumble
- Spaghetti with cauliflower walnut meat sauce
- Strawberry spinach salad with avocado and walnuts

My veganized dish ideas: _____

_____

_____

_____

Wild Rice
1 cup
6.54 grams

- Wild rice and mushroom burger
- Tofu and wild rice stuffed pepper
- Wild rice pilaf

My veganized dish ideas: _____

_____

_____

_____

Actionable Step Towards Going Vegan #7

Think of your favorite fruits and vegetables. Search online how much protein those fruits and veggies typically contain. Aside from eating them raw, can you think of ways to include plant-protein in your meals? Write them down and try them out for your next meal!

Adding blueberries, which offers 0.7 grams of protein per 100 grams, sprinkled on top of homemade buckwheat pancakes is just one mouth-watering example!

Although fruits can be a source of protein, they generally do not provide as much plant protein as vegetables, beans, and nuts.

Some fruits that are considered high-protein fruits include:

- guavas
- avocados
- apricots
- kiwifruit
- blackberries
- oranges
- bananas
- cantaloupe
- raspberries
- peaches

High protein veggies include:

- bok choy
- broccoli
- asparagus
- Brussels sprouts
- artichokes
- collard greens
- cauliflower
- alfalfa sprouts
- spinach

How to get plenty of plant protein:

- Consume adequate calories.

- Eat a variety of whole plant foods with at least 3 servings of legumes per day.

- If you are reducing your calorie intake or are over 60, consider adding a couple more servings of legumes and/or soy based foods to your meals.

How much protein do we *really* need?

On average, adults need to get about **0.83 grams** per kilogram of body weight per day, according to the Institute of Medicine's recommended daily allowance.

The average female needs 46 grams per day. The average male needs 56 grams per day.

Some other sources of plant protein

Plain Soy Milk
1 cup
8 grams

Broccoli Florets
1 cup
3 grams

Peanut Butter
1 tablespoon
4 grams

Buckwheat
1 cup
6 grams

Peas
1/2 cup
4 grams

Nutritional Yeast
1 tablespoon
4 grams

Sweet Potatoes
1 cup
4 grams

Sprouted Whole Grain Bread
1 slice
6 grams

Roasted Unsalted Cashew Nuts
1 cup
21 grams

Plant Powered!
Proteins are made up of amino acids, and we need to consume 9 (known as essential amino acids) out of the 20 total amino acids there are. Our body synthesizes the other 11.

The Protein Myth

Yes, that's right! Plants have protein! And yes, it's possible to get enough protein from a plant-based or vegan diet. In fact, most of us are getting more than enough protein without even trying.

Though plants manufacture all 20 amino acids, not every plant offers every single amino acid. Therefore, it's important to eat an assortment of fruits, vegetables, seeds, whole grains, and nuts to supply essential amino acids required for a healthy body and mind.

One of the strongest animals in the world eats only plants.

By being more aware of your daily food choices, you can certainly get all 9 essential amino acids. They are necessary for us to break down food, help us to grow, repair our body tissue, and perform many other bodily functions.

The question that people *really* need to be asking, rather than wondering where you get your protein from, is **"*...where do you get your fiber from?*"**

Disease Prevention and Reversal

The majority of people who eat a Standard American Diet (SAD) lack enough fiber in their meals. The average American gets about 16 grams of fiber per day — about half of what is suggested by the Institute of Medicine's recommended daily target of 25 grams for women and 38 grams for men.[2]

People in general just aren't eating enough whole fruits, vegetables, beans and legumes, nuts and seeds, and whole grains. It's one main reason why chronic diseases continue to be on the rise worldwide.

Avocados pack 10 grams of fabulous fiber per 1 cup.

Section 10 - Fabulous Fiber

Eating foods rich in fiber is associated with a healthier gut and a lower risk of heart attacks, strokes, high cholesterol, obesity, type 2 diabetes, and even some forms of cancer.

Eating fiber...

- lowers cholesterol levels
- helps control blood sugar levels by slowing the rate of sugar being absorbed into your bloodstream
- improves digestive functions
- boosts the immune system
- decreases inflammation
- can function as prebiotic fiber and feed your "good" bacteria in the intestines
- helps you feel full, which aids in maintaining a healthy body weight
- helps you stay regular and reduces constipation
- cleans your colon by cleaning out bacteria and other buildup in your intestines, reducing your risk for colon cancer
- prolongs longevity by reducing the risk of death from cardiovascular disease and all cancers by helping to flush cholesterol and harmful carcinogens out of your body

Studies have shown that plant-derived foods (which are all 100% cholesterol-free, generally low in saturated fats, and high in fiber, complex carbohydrates, and essential nutrients) have the power to prevent — and even reverse — many chronic health problems.

What is fiber?

Dietary fiber is a non-digestible, calorie-free carbohydrate found only in plant foods.

— **Soluble fiber**: helps to slow the emptying process in our stomachs, which helps you feel fuller. It also helps to control your blood sugar level and get rid of fatty substances such as cholesterol.

Soluble fiber is found in fruits, vegetables, oats, barley and legumes.

— **Insoluble fiber:** absorbs water to help soften the stool and makes it easier for you to have regular bowel movements. This helps to keep your gut healthy and safe from harmful bacteria.

Insoluble fiber is found in whole grain breads and cereals, nuts, seeds, wheat bran, and the skin of fruit and vegetables.

Actionable Step Towards Going Vegan #8

Think of a few of your favorite veggies. Search how many grams of fiber per cup each vegetable contains. Determine how much more fiber you would need to consume if you ate 1 cup of these vegetables every day.

Remember, according to the Institute of Medicine, women need 25 grams of fiber/day and men need 38 grams of fiber/day.

Limiting refined grains — such as white flour, white bread, white pasta, and white rice — and instead choosing whole grains is a great way to boost fiber-rich foods into your diet. Eating whole foods as much as possible is a surefire way to get plenty of it.

Some good sources of fiber include:

- all kinds of beans
- barley
- blackberries
- black-eyed peas
- peas
- raspberries
- prunes
- chickpeas
- artichokes
- whole wheat flour
- bulgur
- bran

Some tips to add more fiber throughout your day:

- Begin your day eating whole-grain cereal or rolled oats and consider adding in some berries, apples, nuts, seeds or bananas.
- Eat whole grains like whole wheat pasta, bulgur wheat or brown rice.
- When buying food, read the labels and make sure it contains at least 2.5 grams of fiber per serving. 5 grams or more per serving is excellent!
- Choose whole-grain breads with at least 2-3 grams of fiber per slice.
- Eating whole fruits rather than drinking fruit juice can offer you as much as twice the amount of fiber.
- If you're not used to eating a lot of fiber, add it gradually into your diet and drink plenty of water so your digestive system has time to adjust.
- Choose raw vegetables over chips. They're great with hummus!
- Throw in some pulses like beans, lentils, or chickpeas onto stews, curries and salads.

Section 11 - There's No Time Like the Present

Whatever your personal reason(s) for going vegan, it should feel good to you. If it's for the animals, you're showing empathy for all sentient beings who have a right to life and freedom. For the environment, you know you're contributing to a greener, more sustainable future so that our younger generations can live in a world where they may flourish. For humans around the world, standing up for those affected by your food and product choices is a show of support and loving concern for others. It also feels amazing for the soul. And of course, your health is one of the most important things in life. Optimum health can give you the best chance to thrive in every moment.

Patience, young grasshopper

For some people, going vegan happens overnight; however, for most others, it happens gradually over time. Dietary choices are usually the first thing people think about when it comes to going vegan. The process of learning new kinds of food, discovering your nutritional needs, reconditioning your mind and body, or weaning off cravings could take months or even years. As time goes on, you will continuously learn more about how it really feels to live a vegan lifestyle. There's a whole lot more we can all learn. So, it's good to practice patience and open-mindedness since there is always something to gain throughout your daily life experiences. Be sure to embrace your challenges and remember to appreciate how far you've already gone.

"Good things take time, as they should. We shouldn't expect good things to happen overnight. Actually, getting something too easily or too soon can cheapen the outcome."

— John Wooden, UCLA Bruins Men's Head Basketball Coach (1948–1975)

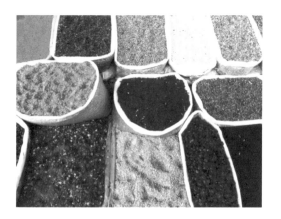

Alright, it's time to explore more!

Going vegan is a fun and exciting time to explore new types of foods and different kinds of cuisines. Trying new kinds of herbs and spices will give your taste buds a whole new mouth-watering, vibrant experience!

It's also a chance to make new friends from all walks of life. As you begin to open your mindset to different cultures and ideas, you'll gain greater self-perspective while observing your own thoughts, feelings, behaviors, and personal motivations.

Section 12 - It's Pantry Time!

Transitioning to a plant-based or vegan diet is going to require some gradual changes. One of those changes includes stocking your pantry and fridge with some whole new types of food. Oh yeah, baby corn!

In the next several pages, you'll see various short lists of items you can add to your pantry broken up into different categories. I share several recommendations to help you make your transition to going meat and dairy free much smoother. This is just a general list of course, and it's up to you to explore more options and learn what suits your taste buds and dietary needs. Remember, you control the power to make choices on every bite of food and sip of drink you take.

Some, or many, of these items may be completely new to you. And that's great! Trying out new foods while learning more about yourself is all part of the journey. This is an exciting time for you. Have some fun with it!

Ready? Here we go!

Breads, Tortillas, Crackers - the simplest forms of bread are generally vegan, containing flour, water, salt, and yeast. In general, flat breads, savory, or dry types of bread are more likely to be vegan, whereas fluffier brioche-types often contain dairy, eggs, or both, making them non-vegan — but there are exceptions. It's important to check the labels of each brand as some also include additional ingredients like sweeteners or fats, both of which can be of animal origin. The most common types of vegan bread include:

Baguette
Ciabatta
Ezekiel
Focaccia
Kosher bread
Pita
Sourdough
Spelt bread
Sprouted grain bread (cinnamon, raisin, sesame, etc.)
Whole grain crackers
Whole grain pita bread
Whole grain tortillas

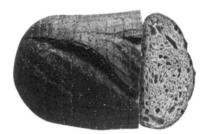

Herbs and Spices - are parts of plants (fresh or dried) that are used to enhance the flavor of foods. They've also been known to preserve foods, cure illness and enhance cosmetics. Herbs come from the leafy and green part of the plant. Spices are parts of the plant other than the leafy bit such as the root, stem, bulb, bark, or seeds. Here are just a handful of common herbs and spices you can add to your pantry. Have a party in your mouth expanding your taste buds!

Anise
Basil
Black pepper
Bay leaf
Cardamom
Cayenne
Cilantro
Cinnamon
Dill
Fennel
Ginger
Lemongrass
Nutmeg
Oregano
Parsley
Rosemary
Saffron
Sesame
Thyme
Turmeric
Vanilla

Cardamom - The Queen of Spices
This exotic spice that is native to India, Bhutan, and Nepal has an intoxicating, rich aroma with complex flavors of sweet floral notes, camphor, mint, lemon, and a hint of pepper. Cardamom is the dried seed pod of a herbaceous perennial plant in the ginger family.

Lemongrass - also called citronella, has a fresh, lemony aroma and a citrus flavor. It's a common ingredient in Thai cooking and can be used as a natural bug repellent.

Turmeric - is a common spice and major ingredient in curry powder. It's also used as a dietary supplement for inflammation; arthritis; stomach, skin, liver, and gallbladder problems; cancer; and other conditions.

Vanilla - comes from the pod of a tropical climbing orchid native to Mexico, and to this day some of the best vanilla beans in the world are produced in Papantla, Mexico.

Actionable Step Towards Going Vegan #9

Start adding some vegan replacements to your pantry. The next few times you go on a grocery run, be sure to pick up several of the items listed in this section. You can use the checklist provided to help you gather the items you need to start "veganizing" some of your favorite dishes. Preparing meals is always more fun (and tastier) when you have the proper ingredients!

Some tips when buying spices:

- Buy them whole. Peppercorns, cinnamon sticks, nutmeg, and other whole varieties will last for several years, while pre-ground spices lose their flavor much faster. You'll need a grinder of some kind. Manual or electric tools will get the job done.

- Search online for specialty shops for any spices that aren't available at your local grocery store. Spice specialists can also help guide you in what you're looking for.

- Keep your spices in a cool, dark place. Avoid using wet utensils or shaking the container over a steaming pan, because any kind of moisture can easily ruin a spice. Glass jars are preferable to plastic since they're not porous. You should also look for containers with well-fitting lids.

- Consider buying in bulk. Having your favorite spices readily available will help make cooking that much easier.

- When purchasing spice blends, carefully read the label. If sugar or salt is listed as the first ingredient, then look for a different brand. Both are cheap fillers that won't give you the most for your money.

- Try creating your own spice blends! Simply mix together your favorite spices to come up with your own personalized signature seasoning.

Dried Fruits - are loaded with micronutrients, fiber, and antioxidants; although, they can be relatively high in calories and natural sugars. Look for labels that show "no sugar added" and "no preservatives added." They're not as nutrient-dense as fresh fruits, but can still be a good, healthy snack when eaten in small amounts.

Apricots
Currants
Cranberries
Figs
Jujube
Medjool dates
Peaches
Prunes
Raisins

Common Vegan Sweeteners - sugars occur naturally in various kinds of plant foods. We get most common sweeteners by processing these plants (such as agave cacti, maple trees, sugar cane, coconut palms, sugar beets and corn) to extract and condense the sugars. Small portions of whole food sweeteners are best for your health.

Agave nectar
Brown rice syrup
Coconut sugar
Date sugar
Lo Han Guo (aka Monk Fruit)
Molasses
Pure Maple Syrup
Stevia
Xylitol

Nut and Butter Seeds - are spreadable foodstuff made by grinding nuts and seeds into a paste. Nut and seed butters have a high content of protein, fiber, and essential fatty acids, and can be used to replace butter or margarine.

Almond butter
Cashew butter
Macadamia nut butter
Peanut butter
Sesame butter
Sunflower seed butter
Tahini (made from sesame seeds)

Plant Oils - are fats taken from a plant, usually from the plants' seeds. Oils are the most calorie-dense food anyone can consume. Personally, I limit consuming oils as much as possible. The best options include organic, unrefined, virgin or extra-virgin. Though these may be considered "healthier" oils, using high amounts of any oil may likely lead to increased body fat and disease promotion. Plant oils are best used in limited amounts for cooking, salad dressings, and/or baking.

Avocado oil
Coconut oil
Flaxseed oil
Hemp seed oil
Olive oil
Peanut oil
Sesame oil
Virgin coconut oil

Plant-Based Milks - are liquids that mix mostly ground nuts and water. Allergic to nuts? No problem. There are a bunch of nut-free alternatives, too. Try to find one that's labeled "unsweetened" or "zero sugar added" and one that's fortified with calcium, vitamin D, and vitamin B12.

Almond milk
Cashew nut milk
Coconut milk
Hazelnut milk
Hemp milk
Oat milk
Rice milk (from brown rice)
Soy milk
Walnut milk

Condiments, Sauces, Spreads - adding vegan flavors to vegan food can help you make the most of your vegan dishes! As always, be sure to read product labels to ensure there are no animal products included.

Balsamic vinegar
BBQ sauce
Black sesame seeds
Cream cheese (non-dairy)
Guacamole
Hummus
Ketchup
Liquid smoke
Mayo (non-dairy)
Mustard
Pasta (marinara) sauce
Peanut sauce
Pesto
Red wine or white wine vinegar
Relish
Rice vinegar
Salsa
Sriracha
Stir-fry sauces, like hoisin and
 black bean sauce
Tamari
Vegan fish sauce
Wasabi

Liquid smoke is a natural product made by condensing the smoke from burning wood. It adds a cook-out like flavoring that can be used for veganizing certain foods such as vegan bacon and tofu jerky.

Sriracha (seer-rah-shah) is a hot chili sauce named for the coastal port city in Thailand from which it originated.

General ingredients include ground chiles, vinegar, garlic, sugar, and salt. People use it on anything and everything they wish to add some heat to.

Wasabi is made from the rhizome of the *Wasabia japonica* plant. Unlike other spicy foods such as chili peppers, which get their spice from their inherent oil capsaicin, the wasabi plant releases a series of spicy vapors when grated. This must be done just before the paste is served since wasabi loses its scent within minutes of being grated.

Nuts and Seeds - botanically speaking, most nuts are the seeds of a fruit. True nuts include chestnuts, acorns, and hazelnuts. Nevertheless, they're not only a healthy, low-maintenance snack, but they're also versatile as ingredients and have been shown to reduce the risk of certain chronic diseases including heart disease and diabetes. Here are just a few of the countless kinds of culinary nuts and seeds you can add to your pantry:

Acorn nuts
Almonds
Brazil nuts
Cashews
Chestnuts
Chilean hazelnuts
Flax seeds
Hemp seeds
Kola nuts
Pecans
Pine nuts
Pistachios
Pumpkin seeds
Sunflower seeds
Walnuts

Beans - are starchy vegetables that are classified as legumes. They're considered one of the most affordable protein sources, making them an invaluable component of the global food supply. They provide a substantial amount of plant-based protein and they're full of fiber, vitamins, minerals, and phytonutrients, which are powerful antioxidants. Choose from a wide variety to try, and keep a decent stash of them in your pantry at all times.

Black beans
Black-eyed peas
Chickpeas (garbanzo beans)
Falafel mix
Fava beans
Kidney beans
Lentils (French, green, red)
Lima or butter beans
Navy beans
Pinto beans
Red kidney beans
Split peas

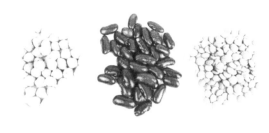

For more descriptions and meal ideas with these pantry recommendations, visit www.goingvegan4goodness.com

Whole Grains - are the seeds of a plant containing all 3 original parts of it: the bran, germ, and endosperm. Be sure to look for the *100% Whole Grain Stamp,* which assures you that all of the grain ingredients are whole grains.

Barley
Black, brown or wild rice
Buckwheat
Bulgur
Corn
Oatmeal
Millet
Quinoa
Rolled oats
Spelt
Whole wheat

Whole Grain Pastas and Noodles - are made from the entire wheat grain. They contain more vitamins, minerals and fiber than regular pasta. The higher amount of fiber content makes it more nutrient dense and filling with even less calories. Be sure to look for the *100% Whole Grain Stamp* or check the list of ingredients. If the first ingredient has the word, "whole" (such as "whole wheat flour" or "whole oats"), it's likely that the product is predominantly whole grain. Remember to read labels carefully and consider finding a brand or two that can be your go-to products.

Brown rice pasta
Corn pasta
Fettuccine
Kamut pasta
Penne
Soba
Spaghetti
Spirals (or Rotini)
Whole grain spaghetti
Udon

Tofu, Tempeh, Seitan - Tofu is made from soybeans similarly to how cheese is made from milk - soy milk is curdled and then pressed into blocks. Tempeh is also made from soybeans, but slightly fermented. Various beans, whole grains, and flavorings are often added as well. Seitan is made entirely out of hydrated gluten, which is the main protein found in wheat. It's sometimes called wheat gluten, wheat meat, wheat protein, or just gluten. All three are popular vegan substitutes for meat because of their high protein content and their unlimited possibilities for flavoring and cooking.

Tofu, extra firm (for stir-frying, oven-baking, grilling)
Tofu, soft (for dips, puddings, baked desserts)
Tempeh (sliced or strips)
Seitan (cubed or diced)

More about tofu, tempeh, and seitan

- **Tofu** – has the fewest calories per serving, making it a good choice for limiting calories; contains the most minerals per calorie; better amino acid profile than tempeh (comparable to seitan).
- **Tempeh** – fermented, and may digest better than tofu; more calorie dense than tofu, which could make it a better option than tofu for gaining weight.
- **Seitan** - highest protein content of all three with a strong amino acid profile. It's very calorie and protein dense, making it a good choice for gaining weight.

Food	Made from	Texture	Taste
Tofu	Soybean curds	Smooth Firmness can be: silken, regular, firm, extra-firm, super-firm	Bland, can taste slightly "beany"
Tempeh	Fermented soy beans	Hard, crumbly, chunky	Earthy, savory, nutty, slightly bitter, mushroom-like
Seitan	Wheat gluten and water	Smooth, but chewy	Mild and savory; can take on different flavors depending on how it's made

Section 13 - Veganizing Your Favorite Dishes

One easy way to start cutting out meat and dairy products is to simply replace those ingredients with plant-based foods - this is what's commonly known as "veganizing."

For example, instead of having cow's milk with your coffee or oats, swap it with soy milk, oat milk or other kind of plant-based milk.

Or, rather than having Beef and Broccoli stir-fry, *veganize it* by having it cooked with tofu instead of beef. Yup, it's that simple! And remember that fish sauce isn't vegan, so you'll need an alternative for that ingredient, which is very common in Asian cuisines.

Being half Thai, I figured I should know how to cook Thai food. One year while visiting my dad in Chiang Mai, Thailand, I took some Thai vegan cooking classes. Replacing typical meats with ingredients such as tofu, mushrooms, and banana hearts turns any meat-based Thai dish into one that's more nutritious and still delicious. *Aroy maak!*

Khao Soi   Yam Hua Plee   Tom Yum Noodle Soup

After a while, you'll realize that "vegan food" is, well, just food! It simply doesn't include any animal products. Eating such innovative, delicious, and nourishing food eventually becomes the norm and wouldn't necessarily require the label of being called vegan; however, during your transition and for the sake of making things easier while ordering food and preparing meals, calling it "vegan" is something that people can relate to.

Pad Thai with tofu

Actionable Step Towards Going Vegan #10

It's time to veganize a few of your favorite dishes! Think of some good eats that you normally like with meat. Chicken Parmesan? Pepperoni pizza? Bacon cheeseburger?

Write down some replacement ingredients for each dish, or simply search online for those recipes and add the keyword "vegan" in front. For example, if you want to veganize omelettes, type in, "vegan omelette recipes." There are countless veganized recipes online for you to choose from. Better yet, get your creative juices flowing and come up with your own veganized versions!

Some vegetables that are commonly substituted for meat include:

- Beans and Legumes - can be used to make hearty soups and stews, black bean burgers, or chickpea "tuna" sandwich
- Mushrooms - provides a "meaty" umami flavor that's great for Portobello burgers, French Dip sandwich, or Mushroom Stroganoff
- Eggplant - offers a rich, versatile meaty taste that can be good for eggplant meatballs, burgers, bacon, or even spiraled eggplant noodles
- Jackfruit - technically a fruit, this stand-in for meat is great for savory dishes including Vegan Philly Cheesesteaks, BBQ Pulled "Pork," or vegan tacos
- Tofu, tempeh, seitan, or TVP - all extremely versatile and are commonly used to make anything you can think of, including crispy tofu nuggets, Kung Pao Tofu, Balsamic BBQ Seitan ribs, Chik'n salads, or even breaded "fish" fillets

Some helpful tips to remember during your transition to going vegan:

- Do your best, be easy on yourself, and stay open-minded along the way.
- Remind yourself of your '*why*' for going vegan. Reviewing your long term goals can be the most powerful driving force for keeping you on track.
- Remember what you are gaining from a plant-based diet or vegan lifestyle as opposed to what you are eliminating.
- Find a friend or two to make vegan meals with or search for vegan meet ups or groups within your local area.
- Buy, borrow, or check out a plant-based/vegan cookbook to get you going.
- Ask for vegan options when dining out. More places are offering them now.
- Visit your local animal sanctuary to remind yourself of your love, respect, and compassion for all animals.

Section 14 - Knowing your 'Vegan Why'

Eating out
Vegan food options are becoming much more readily available these days. You can easily search and locate vegan restaurants right from your own phone. Vegan street fairs and similar events are popping up everywhere, too. They can be the perfect setting to connect with fellow vegans and build your support system. It's also a great way to discover and advocate for local vegan restaurants, chefs, and small businesses.

Popular Vegan Apps
- Vegan Recipe Book App
- Forks Over Knives
- Food Monster
- Vanilla Bean
- Happy Cow
- Yelp

Eating at family gatherings and parties
As you transition to a vegan diet, it can be tempting to eat meat or desserts containing dairy while attending parties. For some, this will be a major challenge and overcoming it may take some time. If (or possibly when) that happens, remember that it's all good! Going with the right mindset and being prepared makes it easier.

Start with why
Your choice to not consume animal products and live a vegan lifestyle may likely be completely opposite from your family, friends, and colleagues. Knowing your *vegan why* and maintaining your vision of achieving your purpose can help you resist potential urges to "take just one bite." With your personal objective as a driving force, you'll learn the process of *how* to adapt and begin to take specific actions needed to carry out your intentions. As a result, you'll gain certainty in *what* it is you do to fulfill your reasons for going vegan. Starting with *why* will help guide you through the entire journey — one that offers some challenges, yet gives a good sense of fulfillment, too. The journey toward achieving your goals can be just as rewarding as accomplishing them.

Preparation tips for food-related gatherings:
- Educate yourself further on the various benefits of not consuming animal products.
- Eat a little bit beforehand to ensure you're not hungry or tempted to eat foods that you may regret eating afterwards.
- Try to find out what kinds of food will be served at the gathering.
- Bring a plant-based/vegan dish or two for everyone (including yourself) to eat and share, if appropriate.
- Eat a variety of meat and dairy-free side dishes if the main dish is animal-based.
- Be confidently prepared to answer questions about what made you decide to stop consuming meat and dairy products.
- Ask yourself if it's in your best interest or worth your time and effort in attending the particular gathering.
- Learn from "minor setbacks" and move on gracefully to the next opportunity.
- Remember your personal *vegan why* and promise yourself you'll do your best.

Actionable Step Towards Going Vegan #11

Write down your thoughts on *WHY* you've chosen to transition towards living a vegan lifestyle.

Do you feel motivated to help save animals from suffering? Do you believe that you can help preserve the planet by not consuming meat and dairy? Do you or a family member suffer from a chronic, preventable lifestyle disease? Every individual has their own reasons and unique purpose. This exercise prepares you to answer to intrigued individuals who tend to ask, "...why did you decide to go vegan?"

Watching a few vegan documentaries and learning more for yourself will help you come up with your own personal reasons. Becoming more educated about our global food systems while witnessing suffering animals who are exploited for human consumption will allow you to gain personal perspective. Yes, some of it may be a bit difficult to watch — but it is important to see the truth behind the animal agriculture industry, as you may develop a greater sense of empathy for all animals and industry workers who are purposefully hidden by the profit-driven corporations that back them.

This can be a time for self-reflection and your willingness to connect with your underlying morals, values, beliefs and actions. Through this, you'll understand how you may relate to other animals, our planet, and your personal health and wellness.

The 2011 documentary, *Forks Over Knives*, was the first vegan documentary that I ever watched. It was an eye-opener for me, and although I didn't become vegan until years later, I did put a temporary halt on eating pork, beef, and chicken. I also stopped drinking cow's milk completely after learning the negative health effects it has on us humans. Plus, cow's milk is meant for baby cows! The influential documentary shares compelling evidence that chronic diseases, including heart disease and type 2 diabetes, can almost always be prevented — and even potentially be reversed — by adopting a whole-food, plant-based diet.

At that time, I was working at UCLA Medical Center as a Certified Clinical Prosthetist and Orthotist. The majority of my patients suffered from complications of diabetes, stroke, and various forms of cancer. Naturally, I felt urged to learn how I can help prevent diseases as opposed to treating them. As my vegan journey continues to evolve, my personal mission has shifted to raising awareness on the multitude of benefits for choosing a plant-based or vegan diet and lifestyle. Soon, you will also discover your own personal *vegan why.*

Section 15 - Ethical Veganism

An individual's choice of diet can be quite the sensitive topic for some people. Because veganism stands for a moral position against harming and exploiting animals, you may come across people who will react defensively when sharing your views.

It's best to tell your reasoning at an appropriate time and in a confident yet non-judgmental manner. Some will exhibit sincere eagerness to learn more about your lifestyle change. Genuinely expressing your beliefs and revealing how going vegan has personally affected your health and/or life can be positively impactful and inspiring.

Cows have a natural life expectancy of 18-25 years; however, the average life span of dairy cows in the US is only 4-6 years old.

"Ethical veganism results in a profound revolution within the individual; a complete rejection of the paradigm of oppression and violence that she has been taught from childhood to accept as the natural order. It changes her life and the lives of those with whom she shares this vision of nonviolence. Ethical veganism is anything but passive; on the contrary, it is the active refusal to cooperate with injustice."

— Gary L. Francione, Animal Rights Activist

In general, vegans do not...
- Wear clothing made from animals including leather, wool, suede, fur, feathers, and silk

- Consume any kind of animal products including butter or cream, eggs, cheese, milk from cows or goats, meat, poultry, lamb, beef, fish, shellfish, shrimp, lobster, or gelatin and honey

- Wear makeup or use similar products that were tested on animals

- Support the exploitation of animals used for entertainment such as in zoos, circuses, horse races, and aquatic theme parks

Staying the course with roadblocks ahead

The majority of people who identify as being vegan commit their best efforts to limit harm, suffering, and exploitation on other animals. It's important to understand that avoiding every single animal product on the market is not realistic in today's world.

Unfortunately, animal-derived products are used for everyday items such as in drywall, clothing, paint, medicine, car tires, and plastics. It's almost impossible to avoid using goods that result from the killing and exploitation of animals. Thus, you can only do what you can to maximize your capabilities without feeling guilt or self-judgement.

As an individual who chooses to live a vegan lifestyle, you have the opportunity to be a voice for those who are silenced and oppressed. Sharing knowledge and spreading awareness on the social injustices against animals and humans can inspire positive change for another individual. The ripple effect can also lead to better health outcomes and positive well-being for your loved ones and community members. By leading a life of self-love and compassion for other humans, animals, and our planet, you can leave an imprint that has the potential to change human and animals' lives for the better.

A few ways to get involved:

- Search online for forums and community groups.

- Join a vegan meet-up or set up a dinner group with like-minded friends in your area.

- Try volunteering at an animal sanctuary near you.

- Locate an animal save group organized by **Animal Save Movement** and bear witness to animals en route to slaughterhouses.

- Locate your local vegan restaurants and street fairs.

- If you're in college, search for vegan, animal rights, and environmental groups to participate in and offer creative outlets for your ideas.

- Locate your nearest **March of Silence** chapter.

- If you're single, join dating apps like *Veggly* and find partners who share your dietary habits and beliefs.

- Search YouTube channels for educational info and inspiring vegan chefs and V-loggers.

Informative YouTube Channels to check out

- Arvin Animal Activist
- avantgardevegan
- Caitlin Shoemaker
- SweetPotatoSoul
- Earthling Ed
- Eight Miles From Home
- Forks Over Knives
- Happy Healthy Vegan
- Joey Carbstrong
- NutritionFacts.org
- Physicians Committee
- Pick Up Limes
- Rich Roll
- Sustainably Vegan
- Tabitha Brown
- The Happy Pear
- Vegan FTA

Actionable Step Towards Going Vegan #12

Visit thesavemovement.org and locate the nearest Animal Save group nearest you. If there isn't one already set up close to you, consider starting a group!

The **Animal Save Movement** started in December of 2010 with the inception of Toronto Pig Save. After witnessing sad and frightened pigs en route to a nearby slaughterhouse in downtown Toronto, co-founder Anita Krajnc made a promise to the pigs to hold a minimum of three animal vigils each week to bear witness. By 2019, over 900 chapters in over 70 countries had been formed.

The Save Movement includes three branches:

1) **Animal Save** - their mission is to hold vigils at every slaughterhouse and to bear witness to every exploited animal.

2) **Climate Save** - their vision is to reverse catastrophic climate change to end animal agriculture and replace fields used for animal feed crops, grazing, and slaughterhouses with forests, wild spaces, and animal sanctuaries.

3) **Health Save** - their mission is to promote and make accessible a plant-based diet to solve the epidemic of preventable diseases and improve the quality of life in our community.

The Save's core values include promoting equality, standing up against all forms of oppression and discrimination, having a moral duty to bear witness, and using a love-based community organizing approach.

Animal vigils focus on animals, while climate and health campaigns help focus on the need for **#FoodSystemChangeNow**. All three branches complement one another to highlight all of the co-benefits of going vegan.

Photo: @bobbysud/@laanimalsave   Photo: @thesavemovement   Photo: @thesavemovement   Photo: @thesavemovement

Section 16 — Resources

Here are just a handful of videos and books to get you started. A simple search online will lead you to many more resources out there. Self-education and self-awareness are two keys to maintaining a healthy and purposeful vegan way of life.

You'll find links to many of these films and books by visiting goingvegan4goodness.com/going-vegan/

Documentaries/Films:
- What The Health
- Forks Over Knives
- Cowspiracy
- Seaspiracy
- Dominion
- Food Matters
- Earthlings
- H.O.P.E.: What You Eat Matters
- The Game Changers
- Vegucated
- Food, Inc.
- Speciesism The Movie
- Fat, Sick & Nearly Dead
- Land of Hope and Glory
- Vanishing of the Bees
- Maximum Tolerated Dose
- Live And Let Live
- Called To Rescue
- The Ghosts In Our Machine
- A Prayer For Compassion
- Eating You Alive
- Empathy

Animal Rights & Nutrition Books:
- Introduction to Animal Rights: Your Child or the Dog? by Gary L. Francione
- Give a Sh*t: Do Good. Live Better. Save the Planet. by Ashlee Piper
- Eating Animals by Jonathan Safran Foer
- Why We Love Dogs, Eat Pigs, and Wear Cows: An Introduction to Carnism by Dr. Melanie Joy
- The Fight for Animal Rights by Jeanne Nagle
- Animalkind: Remarkable Discoveries About Animals and Revolutionary New Ways to Show Them Compassion by Ingrid Newkirk
- Animal Liberation by Peter Singer
- How Not To Die by Michael Greger, M.D.
- The Plant-Based Solution by Joel K. Kahn, M.D.
- Fiber Fueled by Will Bulsiewicz, M.D.
- Plant Over Processed by Andrea Hannemann
- Mastering Diabetes by Cyrus Khambatta, Ph.D. and Robby Barbaro, MPH
- Medical Medium - Life-Changing Foods: Save Yourself and the Ones You Love with the Hidden Healing Powers of Fruits & Vegetables by Anthony William

Actionable Step Towards Going Vegan #13

Schedule a couple of hours aside to watch at least one vegan documentary within the next week or two. Your interest may lead you to watch even more of them, but scheduling your first one is a great way to commit to a day and time and follow through on it.

One good vegan documentary to start off with is the 2017-released *What The Health* film, which you can watch on YouTube. It's the sequel to *Cowspiracy: The Sustainability Secret*, which is another must-see film.

What the Health
2017   Documentary   1h 37m

87% liked this film
Google users

In *What The Health*, filmmaker Kip Andersen uncovers the secret to preventing and even potentially reversing certain chronic lifestyle diseases. As the film unfolds, based on multiple interviews with various health organization representatives, his curiosity leads him to begin investigating why the nation's leading health organizations don't want people to know about it.

Some interesting fast facts from the film
- Two thirds of adults are either overweight or obese[1]
- Most kids by the age of 10 in the US have fatty streaks in their arteries[2]
- Diabetes is not caused by eating a high carbohydrate diet or sugar[3]
- The number one dietary source of cholesterol in America is chicken[4]
- Most of the world's GMO crops are consumed by livestock, with dairy cows consuming most per animal[5]
- The number one source of saturated fat is dairy[6]
- Dairy products contain pus[7]

The film is a bit funny at times, which helps to keep the viewer engaged. It also reveals the eye-opening link between government, big corporations, and America's trillions of dollars' worth of healthcare costs. Many people claim to have switched to a plant-based or vegan diet after watching this particular film. *What The Health* has definitely made an impact on my life. It's one of the first films I recommend to people who express an interest in going vegan.

If you're wondering about popular seafood like tuna, shrimp, and salmon, you'll definitely want to watch the 2021 documentary *Seaspiracy*. This film exposes the very dark and unethical side of commercial fishing and its destructive environmental impact that affects us all.

Section 17 - Alright, Alright. Let's Get Cookin'!

The following pages showcase recipes by a variety of vegan chefs. There are 3 different recipes for each mealtime, plus 3 dessert recipes for those of you who have a sweet tooth like me!

The recipes provided are to help get you started with some common veganized dishes. For even more recipes, simply type in any veganized version you want to try in the search bar of Pinterest or YouTube. You'll come across thousands of meatless and dairy free recipes, along with innovative ways to veganize your favorite meals. You can also visit each of the presented chef's websites or social media pages for more of their recipes and what they have to offer to the community.

Remember, this is also an ideal time to explore your inner foodie, get more creative with new cuisines, and gravitate your taste buds to whole new levels!

"We know we cannot be kind to animals until we stop exploiting them — exploiting animals in the name of science, exploiting animals in the name of sport, exploiting animals in the name of fashion, and yes, exploiting animals in the name of food."

— César Chávez

Some of you may be saying, "This is nice, but I don't cook." Well, if this sounds like you, then maybe it's about that time you do learn and have some fun with it! Transitioning to a vegan lifestyle is all about growth, love, and acceptance. This is your opportunity to challenge yourself and work towards becoming your best self. So go on, you future vegan Top Chef! Take those baby spinach steps outside of your comfort zone and broaden your vegan horizons.

Besides, cooking is not only a valuable life skill, but it also allows you to become more knowledgeable about nutrition and how it effects your body as a whole. The fact is, without your personal health and well-being, you really can't live life abundantly. It's also your gift of conscious love to share with others by providing healthy meals made with kindness and consideration. Paving the path towards living more mindfully, spiritually and not to mention, in much better physical shape is a reward that's truly priceless. Your body, mind, and healthier, glowing skin will thank you for it!

Remember to love your full evolution. Alright then, let's get started with some brekky!

BREAKFAST

Creamy Strawberry & Oat Smoothie Bowl

Recipe from **Susan Cooks Vegan by Susan Pratt.** Susan became vegan in her adult years after she began educating herself on deforestation, over-fishing, ocean plastics, and the inhumane treatment of farm animals. She loves to share her vegan recipes so that you can create wonderful memories with friends and family.

Website: susancooksvegan.com
Instagram: @susancooksvegan

Ingredients
2 frozen ripe bananas chopped into chunks
1 cup rolled oats
1 cup oat milk (plus more if needed)
2 tablespoons hemp hearts
2 dates, pitted
1 heaping cup frozen strawberries
1 teaspoon vanilla extract

Optional toppings:
Dragon fruit, blackberries,
pumpkin seeds, shredded coconut,
hemp hearts, sliced almonds
and edible flowers

Prep time: 3 hours

Total time: 3 hours

Yield: 2 bowls

Photo: Susan Cooks Vegan by Susan Pratt

Instructions
1. Add the oats and the oat milk together to the bowl of your blender and stir. Cover and place in the fridge for at least 3 hours or overnight. This step isn't absolutely necessary — especially if you have a high-powered blender — but it will make the oats easier to blend and give you a creamier and smoother smoothie.

2. When ready to eat, add remaining ingredients and blend on high until thoroughly combined, adding more plant milk if needed.

3. Transfer to a bowl and garnish with the toppings of choice.

Chickpea Omelette

Recipe from **Sister Woman Vegan by Safiya Robinson.** Safiya adopts an intersectional approach to veganism, and her recipes are inspired by West Indian and African American flavors. She wants to make holistic health and wellness more accessible for the Black community with a focus on Black healing, Black joy, and Black futures.

Website: sisterwomanvegan.com
Instagram: @sisterwomanvegan

Ingredients:
3/4 cup chickpea flour
1 cup water
1 teaspoon sea salt
1 teaspoon kala namak*
2 tablespoons lemon juice
1/2 teaspoon baking powder
1/2 teaspoon ground cumin
1/2 teaspoon turmeric
1/2 teaspoon black pepper
1/2 teaspoon smoked paprika
3 tablespoons nutritional yeast

- few sprigs fresh parsley, finely chopped
- 3 chestnut mushrooms, sliced
- handful of spinach
- drizzle avocado oil (or your fave frying oil)

Optional (to serve):
- avocado, sliced
- plantain, sliced and fried
- green salad

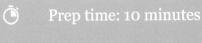
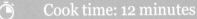

* Kala namak, or black salt is sulfurized so has an eggy taste.

Instructions:

1. Blend together the first 10 ingredients and put aside for 5 minutes.

2. Fry together the mushrooms and parsley until mushrooms are browned. Add the spinach and leave to wilt.

3. In a separate pan, heat the oil and pour the omelette mix in, spread into a pancake shape.

4. When one side is cooked and golden, flip the omelette and cook the other side.

5. Top the omelette with the mushroom and spinach mixture and enjoy with avocado and a salad on the side. Add baked beans for extra protein. Consider throwing in lots of lovely plantains to add a touch of sweetness!

Vegan Chocolate Chip Banana Waffles

Recipe from **hot for food by Lauren Toyota.** Lauren creates vegan versions of popular comfort foods like mac and cheese, burgers, Caesar salad, and even cheesecake — proving that plant-based diets are far from boring.

Website: hotforfoodblog.com
Instagram: @hotforfood

Ingredients:
Waffle batter:
1 banana, mashed
1 1/2 cups all-purpose flour
1 teaspoon baking powder
1 teaspoon cinnamon
1/2 teaspoon sea salt
1 1/2 cups nondairy milk
1/4 cup melted vegan butter
1/2 cup vegan chocolate chips

Serve with:
banana slices, vegan chocolate chips, maple syrup

Instructions:
1. Turn on your waffle iron to heat up.

2. Mash the banana in a large mixing bowl.

3. Add the remaining ingredients and fold together with a spatula to combine. Do not over mix — small lumps in the batter are fine.

4. Spray the waffle iron on both sides with a light coating of oil. Pour half the batter in the center and spread it out to the edges. Close the lid. One batch will take between 7 to 9 minutes to cook through. A good sign is when there is no more steam coming out of the sides of the waffle iron.

Prep time: 15 minutes

Cook time: 18 minutes

Yield: 8 square waffles

Photo: hot for food by Lauren Toyota

5. Remove the waffles with a fork or a skewer from the waffle iron and onto a wire rack. Flip them a couple of times to let them cool. Placing them on a wire rack will allow air to circulate around the waffles so they remain crispy.

6. Serve with extra banana slices, chocolate chips, and maple syrup.

LUNCH

Rainbow Chickpea Curry Bowl

Recipe from **Plant-based Amor by Mike Sincere and Jezzy B.** The Vegan couple are two Los Angeles based DJ's who love spinning and cooking cruelty-free dishes from the heart.

Website: plantbasedamor.com
Instagram: @plantbasedamor

Ingredients
1 cup of cooked chickpeas
1/2 cup of cooked quinoa
1/2 cup of shredded purple cabbage
1/4 cup of coconut milk
1/2 cup of diced red bell pepper
1/2 cup of chopped spinach
2 chopped spring onions
1/2 cup of chopped baby carrots
1 teaspoon of curry powder
1/2 teaspoon smoked paprika
1/2 teaspoon of turmeric
1/2 teaspoon of cumin
1 teaspoon of granulated garlic
1 teaspoon of salt
dash of black pepper

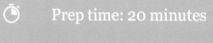
Prep time: 20 minutes

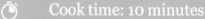
Cook time: 10 minutes

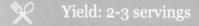
Yield: 2-3 servings

Instructions:
1. Sauté cooked chickpeas with coconut milk and spices on medium heat for 4 minutes. Let cool until slightly warm.

2. In a large bowl, combine all ingredients and top with some avocado!

Photo: Plant-based Amor

JACKFRUIT "PULLED PORK SANDWICHES" WITH CREAMY-TANGY SLAW

Recipe from **To Live For Vancouver by Erin Ireland.** Erin is a passionate food reporter for *CTV Morning Live, BC Living Magazine* and her website, which serves to connect Vancouverites with the most delicious and ethically-sourced food in the city. She is also a seasoned home cook and baker, food stylist, and food photographer.

Website: tolivefor.ca
Instagram: @erinireland

Ingredients:
For the jackfruit pulled pork:
1 large can jackfruit (net weight: 482g, in water, not syrup)
2 large garlic cloves (minced)
1 tablespoon olive oil
1/3 cup BBQ sauce (I used Organicville's)
1 tablespoon onion powder
1 teaspoon smoked paprika
1 teaspoon fresh-ground pepper
2 tablespoons white vinegar
3/4 teaspoon Himalayan salt

Prep time: 15 minutes

Cook time: 10 minutes

Yield: 2-3 servings

For the slaw:
1/4 head large purple cabbage (finely shredded)
3 tablespoons vegan mayo (I used Hellmann's)
1 teaspoon grainy mustard (or more if you like it)
1 tablespoon red wine vinegar
1 teaspoon fresh-ground pepper
3/4 teaspoon Himalayan salt

For the bun and garnishes:
2-3 hamburger buns (I used PIKANIK's)
2-3 tablespoons vegan mayo (1 tablespoon per bun)
2-3 teaspoons grainy mustard
3 handfuls greens (I used radish sprouts from my Urban Cultivator)

Photo: To Live For Vancouver by Erin Ireland

Instructions:

1. Using a mandolin, shred your cabbage into skinny bits that are easy to chew. Transfer cabbage to a bowl and add mayo, mustard, vinegar, salt and pepper. Toss to combine. Set aside in fridge while you make your pulled jackfruit.

2. Heat oil in a pan and add minced garlic. Drain your can of jackfruit, and add it to the pan. Using a wooden spatula, mash the jackfruit so it breaks apart.

3. Add spices, BBQ sauce and vinegar to your jackfruit and mix to combine so it's evenly coated with flavor.

4. Time to build your sandwich: toast your buns and add mayo to one side, mustard to the other. Load on your jackfruit, followed by slaw. Top with a handful of greens and enjoy.

Chef Del Sroufe's Sloppy Joes

Recipe from **China Study Family Cookbook by Chef Del Sroufe.** He is also the author of *Forks Over Knives: The Cookbook* and *Better Than Vegan*, the story of his struggle with weight loss and gain, and how he lost over 200 pounds on a low fat, plant-based diet.

Website: chefdelsroufe.com
Instagram: @chefdelsroufe

Ingredients
1 medium onion, finely chopped
1/2 green bell pepper, finely chopped
1 celery stalk, finely chopped
2 cloves garlic, minced
2 cups cooked wheat berries (see tip below)
1 15-ounce can tomato puree
1/3 cup date puree (recipe below)
1/4 cup ketchup
1 tablespoon vegan Worcestershire sauce or tamari
Sea salt and black pepper
6 whole grain hamburger buns

 Prep time: 10 minutes

 Cook time: 20 minutes

 Yield: 6 sandwiches

Instructions
1. Sauté the onion, bell pepper, and celery in a medium-size skillet over medium heat for 7 to 8 minutes. Add water 1 to 2 tablespoons at a time to keep the vegetables from sticking to the pan. Add the garlic and cook for another minute.

2. Add the cooked wheat berries, tomato puree, date puree, ketchup, and Worcestershire sauce, and cook, stirring occasionally, until the sauce thickens (about 10 minutes). Season with sea salt and black pepper to taste.

Photo: Forks Over Knives: the Cookbook by Chef Del Sroufe

3. Place the bottom halves of each hamburger bun on a work surface and top with some of the filling. Place the tops of the buns on the sandwiches and serve.

RECIPE TIP

Wheat berries can be found at natural food stores and online retailers. To cook them, combine 2/3 cup wheat berries and 2 cups water in a small saucepan. Bring the water to a boil over medium-high heat, reduce the heat to medium, cover, and cook for 50 to 60 minutes, until the water is absorbed and the wheat berries are tender.

Date Puree

I use this puree in a lot of dessert recipes. It is a great way to get your family off processed sugar.

Makes 3 cups

2 cups pitted dates
2 cups water

1. Combine the dates and water in a small saucepan. Cover and cook over medium heat until the dates are tender, about 10 minutes. Drain and reserve the cooking water.

2. Puree the dates in a blender, adding just enough water to make a creamy consistency. Let cool to room temperature, then store in an airtight container for up to a week.

RECIPE TIP

Add as little water as possible to the dates to concentrate the sweetness in the puree. Date puree is not a 1:1 replacement for sugar and, to the newbie, may not taste as sweet. If you are trying to use this date puree instead of sugar in your favorite recipes, you may need to cut back a bit on the liquid in your recipe, and it may take a little experimentation to figure out exactly how much date puree to use.

Actionable Step Towards Going Vegan #14

Think about someone in your family or circle of friends who is suffering from type 2 diabetes or a form of cardiovascular disease. Let them know about your newfound knowledge that a whole-food, plant-based diet has the potential to reverse these two lifestyle diseases.

There is plenty of evidence-based research showing that lifestyle changes, particularly diet, can be highly effective in preventing, treating, and even reversing type 2 diabetes and heart disease.

It's been shown that a whole-food, plant-based diet consisting of legumes, whole grains, fruits, vegetables, and nuts with very limited or no intake of refined foods or animal products can not only prevent diabetes, but treat it, too.[1] Eating plant-based foods also goes hand-in-hand with treating associated cardiovascular disease, which is the leading cause of death in the United States and a common co-morbidity (two illnesses or diseases occurring in the same person at the same time for individuals with type 2 diabetes.

In addition, it can lower heart disease risk factors including obesity, hypertension (high blood pressure, hyperlipidemia (high levels of fat in the blood, and inflammation. Likewise, a whole-food, plant-based diet can reduce the risk of cancer, the second leading cause of death in the United States.[2]

There are countless stories of people just like you, me, and our own family members who have gotten off their diabetes and heart related medications. How did they did do it? They simply chose plants over pills as their natural form of medicine. I personally know a handful of individuals who have decreased, and in some cases, eliminated their daily dose of medications by going on a completely whole-food, plant-based diet. If they can do it, chances are that our own friends and family members can, too.

Please note that changing to a plant-based diet can lead to a significant and abrupt decrease in your blood sugar and blood pressure relatively quickly, especially if you are taking medications for these conditions. Please consult with your physician or other qualified healthcare professional when changing your diet.

DINNER

Maple Balsamic Roasted Brussel Sprouts

Recipe by **Haile Thomas**, an international speaker, wellness and compassion activist, vegan food and lifestyle content creator, the youngest to graduate from the Institute for Integrative Nutrition as a Certified Integrative Nutrition Health Coach (at age 16), and the founder and CEO of the non-profit HAPPY (Healthy, Active, Positive, Purposeful, Youth).

Website: hailevthomas.com
Instagram: @hailethomas

Ingredients:
3-4 cups Brussels sprouts, halved
1/3 cup olive oil
1/3 cup balsamic vinegar
1/3 cup maple syrup
Himalayan sea salt to taste
1 tablespoon fresh thyme

Toppings:
Pepitas (pumpkin seeds)

Prep time: 10 minutes

Cook time: 40 minutes to 1 hour

Yield: 4 servings

Photo: Haile Thomas

Instructions
1. Preheat oven to 400 degrees F. Lightly grease a baking sheet with 1/2 tablespoon olive oil. Set aside.

2. In a small/medium sized bowl, combine olive oil, balsamic vinegar, and maple syrup until well incorporated.

3. Place halved Brussels sprouts on your prepared baking sheet and drizzle maple balsamic mixture on top, tossing to fully coat. Sprinkle with salt to taste and fresh thyme.

4. Roast in the oven for 40 minutes - 1 hour or until golden and crisp, yet tender, piercing it with a fork. Remove from oven and sprinkle with pepitas and dried cranberries. Enjoy as a festive side or on its own!

Sweet Potato & Lentil Stew

Recipe from **Plant Based Nordic by Linus Skaring.** Linus started his vegan journey in 2017. For him, the journey is not about "being vegan" or not, it's about taking a step towards a more sustainable, healthy, and ethical way of living, where every step counts. Linus is a certified nutritionist who specializes in plant-based nutrition. His goal is to teach both vegans and people who are interested in a vegan diet the basics of nutrition so that they can implement that knowledge into their everyday life.

Website: plantbasednordic.com
Instagram: @plantbasednordic

Ingredients
1 cup red lentils, dry
1 large sweet potato
1 yellow onion
1 bell pepper
Handful of mushrooms
2 cloves of garlic
1/2 red chili
1/4 cup of canned tomatoes
2 tablespoon tomato paste
1 - 1 1/4 cup of coconut milk
1 stock cube
1/2 teaspoon curry
1/2 teaspoon cumin
1/2 teaspoon paprika powder
1/2 teaspoon cayenne pepper
1/2 tablespoon canola oil
2 1/2 cups of water

Options:
Kale
Legumes
Ginger

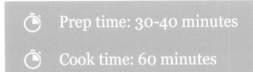
Prep time: 30-40 minutes

Cook time: 60 minutes

Yield: 3-4 servings

Photo: Plant Based Nordic by Linus Skaring

Instructions:

1. Set the oven at 225 C/435 F. First, peel the sweet potato, then use a fork to poke holes all over the surface of it so that the liquid can come out of it. Place it in the oven for about 35-50 minutes depending on its size. The sweet potato is ready once it is soft throughout.

2. You can start preparing the stew when the sweet potato has been in the oven for about 30 minutes. Take out your remaining ingredients and chop up your vegetables. Use a large size saucepan and set stove to medium-high heat.

3. Throw the minced onion into the saucepan and let it get some color before adding the remaining vegetables, garlic, and chili, along with the seasoning. Stir well then lower heat to medium.

4. Let it brew together for a short time before you add the lentils, canned tomato, tomato paste, vegetable stock, and water. Let it boil up on high heat and then immediately lessen the heat down to low temperature.

5. Leave everything for about 15 minutes or until the lentils have softened. Finally, finish the stew by mashing the sweet potato into the pot (without peel) with the coconut milk.

Creamy Pesto

Recipe by **Charlie Fyffe**, a vegan chef and activist. While majoring in Leadership and Social Change at UC Berkeley, he founded Charlie's Brownies, now an all vegan and organic, allergen friendly baked goods brand. In 2019, he co-founded Vegan AF Events and in 2020, launched the *Vegan Recipe Book App*, a digital platform for sharing his weekly recipes and teaching plant-based cooking.

Website: veganrecipebook.app
Instagram: @charlie_fyffe & @CharliesBrownies

Hemp Seed Pesto
1 1/4 cups fresh basil
1/2 cup hulled hemp seeds
1/2 cup sprouted pumpkin seeds
1 tablespoon + 1 tsp umeboshi paste
1 tablespoon + 1 tsp chickpea miso
1 cup avocado oil
1/2 teaspoon dried parsley
1/8 teaspoon mustard powder
1/8 teaspoon fine sea salt
Pinch lemon zest
1/2 teaspoon Moringa powder (optional)

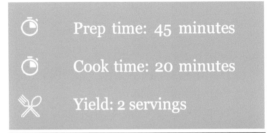

- Prep time: 45 minutes
- Cook time: 20 minutes
- Yield: 2 servings

Instructions:
1. Remove large stems from the basil.

2. Add all ingredients into a high powered blender and blend on high for 30 seconds until well combined.

Photo: Charles Fyffe

Substitutions: Basil contributes a really special and classic flavor to the pesto. If you do not have enough basil, you can substitute a portion of it or all of it with other fresh greens such as arugula, kale, and/or carrot tops. Hemp seeds contribute healthy omega fatty acids to this pesto. If you do not have hemp seeds, you can substitute with pumpkin seeds or soaked and drained peeled tiger nuts. Umeboshi paste is both salty and sour with a deep flavor profile making for the perfect substitute for Parmesan cheese. Umeboshi is an essential ingredient in this pesto. It can be purchased at health food markets, Asian markets, and online.

Notes: Pesto is great as a dip or bread spread and excellent in sandwiches. It adds depth to cheese plates and is great as a pasta sauce.

Storage: Stored in the fridge, this pesto will last for 1 week. Stored in the freezer, this pesto will last for 3 months.

Creamy Pesto Penne
1 cup gluten free penne noodles
1/4 cup pesto sauce
1/2 cup baby greens (spinach, arugula, tatsoi, Swiss chard)
1/4 cup sun dried tomatoes (in oil or dry)
Lemon
Fine sea salt
Parsley (dried)
Oregano
Black pepper
Crushed red pepper
Hulled hemp seeds
Sautéed broccolini (optional)
Sliced avocado (optional)
Vegan Parmesan (optional)
Spicy aioli (optional)

Instructions
1. Slice sun dried tomatoes julienne. Set aside.

2. If adding broccolini, steam broccolini for a few minutes to soften. In a large skillet, sauté with light avocado oil and a dash of umeboshi paste on medium heat for a few minutes. Finish with a touch of fine sea salt and a squeeze of lemon. Set broccolini aside and save oiled skillet for step 4.

3. Prepare penne noodles. Cook al dente. Drain noodles.

4. In the large skillet, pan fry noodles in pesto sauce, baby greens, and sun dried tomatoes on medium-low heat. Season with additional salt to taste.

5. Plate. Add broccolini and sliced avocado if using, squeeze some citrus, and top with dried parsley, oregano, black pepper, hemp seeds, and crushed red pepper.

6. If you are feeling saucy, drizzle aioli over the whole plate before adding your dry toppings. You can make a quick aioli by stirring vegan mayo with your favorite hot sauce and a tiny bit of lemon juice or water. Add liquid to mayo until desired consistency is reached.

7. Serve immediately and enjoy!

Additions: Peas, cherry tomatoes, sautéed zucchini, mushrooms, and many other vegetables will work as an addition to this plate. Topping this dish with vegan Parmesan is also very nice.

DESSERTS

Miyoko's Phenomenally Vegan New York Style Cheesecake

Recipe from **Miyoko's Creamery by Miyoko Schinner** - "the Queen of vegan cheese" is the industry leader on making 100% non-dairy cheese, butter, and other goodies from organic, real foods like nuts, legumes, and other plant-based ingredients.

Website: miyokos.com
Instagram: @miyokoscreamery

Ingredients

The Crust:
1/2 cup walnuts
3/4 cup rolled oats
3 tablespoons organic sugar
1/3 cup melted Miyoko's European-Style Cultured Vegan Butter
1 teaspoon vanilla
1/2 teaspoon cinnamon
1/4 teaspoon nutmeg

 Prep time: 15 minutes

 Bake time: 50 minutes

 Yield: 4 servings

The Cheesecake:
2 lbs. Miyoko's Plainly Classic Vegan Cream Cheese
1 cup organic sugar
3/4 cup organic coconut cream
1/4 cup organic cornstarch or arrowroot
1/4 cup maple syrup
1 tablespoon agar powder
1 tablespoon vanilla extract
2 teaspoons lemon zest

Photo: Miyoko's Creamery

Instructions

1. Preheat the oven to 350 degrees F.

2. Prepare the crust. Combine all of the crust ingredients in a food processor and process until crumbly. Then press into the bottom of an 8 or 9 inch spring form pan lined with parchment.

3. Place all cheesecake ingredients in a food processor and process until smooth and creamy, about 1 minute. Alternatively, place all but the last three ingredients in a large bowl and use an electric mixer or a wooden spoon to mix well.

4. Add the final three ingredients – the agar, vanilla extract, and lemon zest, and mix well.

5. Pour cheesecake mixture onto the prepared crust. Bake for about 50 minutes, until lightly browned on top.

6. Let cool completely, then place in the refrigerator for several hours or overnight before serving.

7. Enjoy plain, or top with your favorite seasonal berries and a light sprinkle of powdered sugar.

Berry Oat Bake

Recipe from **Plant Strong by Rip Esselstyn**. Plant Strong offers a one-week, self- guided journey through a whole foods, plant-based lifestyle. They also have a great private community where you can connect with others who are inspired to improve their health and prevent certain diseases.

Website: plantstrong.com
Instagram: @ripesselstyn

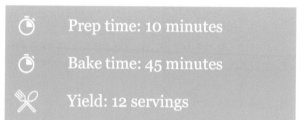

Prep time: 10 minutes

Bake time: 45 minutes

Yield: 12 servings

Ingredients
4 cups old-fashioned rolled oats
3 cups unsweetened applesauce
2 cups unsweetened almond milk (or water)
2 cups raspberries (frozen of fresh)
1 cup sweet cherries (frozen or fresh)
3 tablespoons flax meal
1 tablespoon cinnamon
1/4 cup walnuts (optional)

Instructions
1. Preheat oven to 400 degrees Fahrenheit.

2. In a 9x13 pan, mix the oats, applesauce, berries, cherries, plant-milk, and flax together and top with the cinnamon and walnuts. Then bake for 45 minutes or until the top is slightly browned.

Try this with peaches and blueberries or bananas and strawberries!

Photo: Plant Strong by Rip Esselstyn

Shake, Dalmatian Shake!

Recipe from **The Bizerkeley Vegan by Erika Hazel.** Erika is a Bay Area food critic and blogger, a vegan entrepreneur and a passionate event planner. Aside from traveling around the U.S., she organizes galas, trips, parties, fundraisers, food festivals in and around Berkeley, California.

Website: thebizerkeleyvegan.com
Instagram: @bizerkeleyvegan

Ingredients
1 1/2 cups vegan vanilla ice cream, use your favorite
1 teaspoon vanilla extract
1 tablespoon powdered sugar (optional)
About 3-5 chocolate sandwich cookies of your choice
About 1/4 - 1/2 cup non-dairy milk

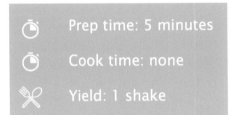

Prep time: 5 minutes

Cook time: none

Yield: 1 shake

Instructions

1. Start by putting vanilla ice cream in bottom of blender. Pour non-dairy milk on top and let the ice cream soften up a bit. The ratio should be 4:1 for the ice cream and milk.

2. Next pour in about 1/2 teaspoon of vanilla extract

3. Add 1 tablespoon of Powdered sugar

4. Once softened up, pulse or blend for about 10 seconds until it is still thick and creamy but not watery (unless you like yours thin!).

5. Once ice cream mixture is 80% done, drop in crumbled Oreos/Joe Joe's in your preferred size. I like mine chunky but you can crush yours in a Ziploc bag or with your fingers to make them smaller.

Photo: The Bizerkeley Vegan
by Erika Hazel

6. Blend in Oreos, but make sure to keep the mixture thick! If it gets too thin, add in more ice cream.

7. Once everything is mixed together, you will have a white milkshake speckled with black cookies to make it look like the 101 Dalmatian aesthetic we were going for!

Actionable Step Towards Going Vegan #15

It's time to host a potluck dinner - vegan style of course! Now that you've gained much more knowledge and awareness about transitioning to a vegan lifestyle, why not share some of that plant-powered wisdom with your family and friends? This is also the ideal time to show off some of your plant-based cooking skills!

I'm so excited you've made it here! This is where your journey into living a vegan lifestyle really begins to skyrocket. Preparing and hosting a home cooked meal and dinner party that's inspired by unconditional love and compassion for others (including animals) is one of the greatest gifts you can give to anyone. This is also a reflection of your love and respect for our planet.

Putting in your best efforts to serve food that doesn't require harm to any animal, is healthy, and delicious is a direct transfer of your positive energy, love, and light into the lives of those who are fortunate to be within your circle.

For this final **Actionable Step Towards Going Vegan**, you will be cooking Rip Esselstyn's famous "Raise The Roof" Sweet Potato Lasagna. In the 2011 *Forks Over Knives Presents The Engine 2 Kitchen Rescue with Rip Esselstyn* documentary, Rip was featured as a firefighter in the Austin Fire Department. The film reveals how he discovered dangerously high cholesterol levels among his fellow firefighters. He showed that the number one killer of firefighters in the line of duty deaths was, of all things, heart disease. This led him to create a revolution of dietary change that resulted in improving the health of his fellow comrades.

As an identical twin whose brother was a firefighter for the Los Angeles City Fire Department at the time I watched this film, this eye-opening reality really hit close to home. It was this documentary that kick started my journey towards plant-based eating for the purpose of improving my and my family's health. Although it took me a couple years to gradually make the full transition to going vegan, I learned about this recipe and it gave me the inspiration to cook my very first meat and dairy free lasagna for some friends. It was a big hit, and I'm sure it will be with your friends, too!

Alright, it's time to set up a dinner party and prepare this delicious plant-based lasagna for you and a few of your friends. Invite them over and ask each person to bring an appetizer such as a dinner salad, hummus and chips, or a fruit platter. Let them know about your new journey towards living a vegan lifestyle and how much you would love to prepare this meal for them!

Rip Esselstyn's Raise The Roof Sweet Potato & Vegetable Lasagna

If this is your first time ever making lasagna, the prep time may feel a bit long. It did for me, at least. I can assure you that it's well worth the time and effort. Meat-eaters and non-meat-eaters alike that I've served this to agree that it's delicious. Enjoy the process (and progress) and have fun at your dinner party!

Recipe from **Plant Strong by Rip Esselstyn.** As the founder of Engine 2, Rip develops and implements a range of programs and events geared toward education, inspiring, and nurturing plant-strong living for individuals, families, and organizations all over the world. Rip is an executive producer of *The Game Changers* film, a *New York Time's* Bestselling Author, and a 2019 world record holder in the 200 meter backstroke for men ages 55-59.

Website: plantstrong.com
Instagram: @ripesselstyn

Ingredients:
1 onion, chopped
1 small head of garlic, chopped or pressed
1 cup mushrooms, sliced
1 head broccoli, chopped
2 carrots, chopped
2 red bell peppers, seeded and chopped
1 can corn, rinsed and drained
1 package firm tofu
1/2 teaspoon cayenne pepper
1 teaspoon oregano
1 teaspoon basil
1 teaspoon rosemary
2 jars pasta sauce
2 boxes whole grain lasagna noodles
16 ounces frozen spinach, thawed and drained
2 sweet potatoes, cooked and mashed
6 Roma tomatoes, sliced thin
1 cup raw cashews, ground

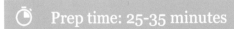

Prep time: 25-35 minutes

Bake time: 45 minutes

Yield: 10-12 servings

Photo: Plant Strong by Rip Esselstyn

Instructions:

1. Preheat oven to 400 degrees. Sauté the onion and garlic on high heat for 3 minutes in a wok or nonstick pan. Add the mushrooms and cook until the onions are limp and the mushrooms give up their liquid. Place the mushrooms, onion, and garlic into a large bowl, saving the mushroom liquid in the pan.

2. Sauté the broccoli and carrots for 5 minutes and add to the mushroom bowl. Sauté the peppers and corn until just beginning to soften and add to the vegetable bowl.

3. Drain the silken tofu by wrapping in paper towels. Use your hands to crumble the tofu in the towels and mix into the vegetable bowl. Add spices to the mixture and combine.

To assemble the lasagna:

1. Cover the bottom of a 9" x 13" casserole dish with a layer of pasta sauce. Add a layer of noodles. Cover the noodles with sauce. This helps the noodles cook in the oven, saving time and energy.

2. Spread the vegetable mixture over the sauced noodles. Cover with a layer of noodles and another dressing of sauce. Add the spinach to the second layer of sauced noodles. Cover the spinach with the mashed sweet potatoes.

3. Add another layer of sauce, the final layer of noodles, and a last topping of sauce. Cover with foil and bake in the oven for 45 minutes.

4. Remove the foil, sprinkle with the cashews or nutritional yeast, and return to the oven for another 15 minutes. Let the lasagna sit for 15 minutes before serving.

Section 18 - Compassion: A Key Ingredient

As you can see, going vegan is not just considered a type of diet by many. It can be viewed as a daily lifestyle practice of consciousness, self-awareness, non-violence and purposeful living. It's an understanding that we are all sentient beings who strive for the same things in life - food, water, shelter, love, happiness, and freedom.

Living vegan acknowledges the abusive and destructive impact on all species and our precious planet. It's choosing to become a protector of the innocent ones who cannot defend themselves. This includes our Mother Earth who provides us with her home, opportunities to explore our resourceful planet, and our very own breath.

I believe compassion is a key ingredient to understanding that who, what, why, and where you eat is vital to your health and to helping others in need. It encourages self-reflection on your physical, mental, emotional, and spiritual needs - a worthy practice in discovering your personal life purpose. When our heart is filled with love and compassion, we may act in ways that help relieve the sufferings of others. Compassionate empathy extends beyond understanding others and experiencing their emotions. It can help transform discerning thoughts into intentional actions.

In the end, it's all about kindness

Nourishing yourself by eating well, exercising often, getting good quality sleep, and maintaining healthy social relationships are all forms of loving kindness. Also, staying mindful about how you treat yourself is so important for overall health and well-being. It all starts with what you feed your mind, body, and soul. Eating nutritious foods is considered one of the greatest forms of self-love, self-discipline, and self-respect. Once you adopt this mindset of greater self-awareness, everything begins to shift.

Possessing a higher sense of emotional empathy for other sentient beings and our planet can make all the difference. With the capability to share your feelings and build connections with non-human animals, your dietary choices (and overall lifestyle choices) will side with being kinder and more understanding each day. It's these daily solo acts of kindness that can collectively contribute to a better world - one in which all beings can be free to live in harmony.

Not consuming animal products is the first step in eliminating the negative energies of pain, fear, suffering, and violence associated with the production of meat and dairy. Choosing foods that are whole and plant-based can provide you with the essential nutrients to live life optimally. You benefit by gaining a practical understanding of your health and the humanitarian impacts of your dietary choices. Remember, you're not just being kind to yourself. In essence, you are showing solidarity while supporting the millions of affected humans and animals who wish for peace, love, and happiness just like you.

Living your best vegan life(style)

We all know that change is good — but we also know that altering our daily habits can be difficult and discouraging at times. Countless hurdles and setbacks must be anticipated while pursuing lifestyle change. Relapse is all too common, perhaps even inevitable. It's good to view these challenges as an integral part of one's life journey. I whole-heartedly believe that there's no such thing as failure, only lessons learned. I personally view them as directional steps towards carrying out our true life purpose.

The good news is that you've surpassed the willingness to modify your dietary habits and have already taken progressive action. You faced some barriers and overcame them. And that makes you awesome! Your intention towards living your best vegan life has been set forth into the universe. Oh yeah, baby yams! Finally, you've set your meaningful goals and underlying purpose in *going vegan 4 goodness*.

This is your moment, your chance, and your vision for a better self and a kinder world. It's important to find what works best for you, as there are infinite paths toward living a vegan way of life. I hope you take the information you've learned here as a stepping stone and guiding light into discovering what best suits your body and your world.

Remember that constant change is a gradual process (and progress) without a set timeline. It requires patience and persistence. Having an open mind and the ability to adapt and accept unexpected challenges is helpful in the journey. As you continue to build supportive relationships that encourage your lifestyle change, you will surely reap positive health outcomes while inspiring others to follow your lead. Once you are able to overcome the old, unhealthy habits and re-train certain preconceived thoughts, your motivation to sustain healthier habits will continually flow with ease.

I thank you for giving your time and energy into reading *Going Vegan 4 Goodness*. I wish you all the best with full faith in you to continue shining your courageous light. Families, the animals, our planet, and our future generations will surely thank you, too.

Section 19 - Glossary of Common Terms

Bearing witness: Seeing and recognizing the suffering of animals who are arriving to a slaughterhouse. It refers to being present with them while showing comfort and care. Those who bear witness usually provide the animals water while displaying compassion during their final hours of life.

Bykill: Marine animals unintentionally caught in nets and killed via commercial fishing, e.g. dolphins caught and killed when fishing for tuna or salmon.

Cruelty-Free: Indicates that products do not contain animal products and were not tested on animals.

Dead zone: An area of an ocean (or lake) that has too little oxygen to support marine life; it is hypoxic. This is a natural phenomenon that has been increasing in shallow coastal and estuarine areas as a result of human activities. Dead zones occur around the world, but primarily near areas where heavy agricultural and industrial activity spill nutrients into the water and compromise its quality accordingly.

Factory farming: A system of rearing livestock using intensive methods by which poultry, pigs, or cattle are confined in small areas under strictly controlled conditions to produce a large amount of meat, eggs, or milk as cheaply as possible.

Flexitarianism: A type of diet that is more about adopting a healthier eating habit by including more vegetarian meals over animal-based meals.

Fruitarianism: A controversial diet that is a subset of raw veganism and involves a diet consisting of about 75% raw fruit by weight, and 25% nuts and seeds. The health of a fruitarian diet is not supported by scientific evidence, and the diet increases the risk of nutritional deficiencies such as vitamin B12, calcium, iron, zinc, Omega-3, and protein.

Gluten-Free: A label that indicates that the product does not contain gluten, which is a general name for the proteins found in wheat, rye, barley, and triticale.

GMOs: Genetically Modified Organisms, which are organisms (plants, animals and microorganisms) whose genetic material (DNA) has been altered in a way that does not occur naturally by mating and/or natural recombination.

Hatchery: A place where eggs are hatched; especially, a place for producing poultry on a large scale, or a place for hatching fish to restock streams.

Lacto-vegetarianism: Lacto-vegetarians ("lacto" from the Latin root word for milk) do consume dairy products but cut out eggs from their diets. Lacto-vegetarian diets are popular with many followers of the Eastern religious traditions such as Hinduism, Jainism, Buddhism, and Sikhism.

Mock Meat and Dairy: Food products that have the look, texture and taste of animal meat and dairy products but are vegan.

Nooch: Nickname for nutritional yeast, a common vegan food staple that replicates the taste of cheese when added to recipes.

Nori (nor-ee): Japanese name for an edible seaweed commonly used for vegan sushi rolls.

Nutritional Yeast: A yeast grown on molasses that is heated (to deactivate the yeast), harvested, washed, and packaged as flakes or powder. Also known as nooch.

Organic: Refers to a set of practices used by growers that seek to promote ecological balance and conserve biodiversity by not using pesticides, fertilizers, irradiation, industrial solvents, or synthetic food additives.

Outreach: Speaking to non-vegans in the wider public as a form of activism. An 'outreach event' may involve leafleting, talking to strangers, and engaging in fruitful conversations with them.

Ovo-lacto-vegetarianism/Vegetarianism: When someone says they're vegetarian, this is what they usually mean. General vegetarians do not consume meat of any kind, but do consume both dairy and egg products. This can be a great starting point if you want to gradually transition towards living a vegan lifestyle. It is a relatively easy diet to follow with adequate calcium and protein intake.

Ovo-vegetarianism: "Ovo" is the Latin word for egg. This type of vegetarianism allows for the consumption of eggs, but not dairy products. The driving motivations are based on the perceived cruelty of the industrial practice of keeping a cow constantly lactating and slaughtering unprofitable male calves, as opposed to egg-laying hens, which produce unfertilized eggs for consumption.

Pescatarianism: A pescatarian's diet includes fish and seafood in addition to vegetarian foods such as beans, vegetables, fruits, dairy, and grains.

Processed Food: Food that is packaged in boxes, cans or bags, and often contains additives, artificial flavorings, and other chemical ingredients.

Raw: Uncooked and unprocessed food, mostly fruit, vegetables, nuts and seeds.

Raw Veganism: A type of vegan diet that excludes all food and products of animal origin, as well as food cooked at a temperature above 48°C (118°F). The idea is that heating food destroys its nutrients and natural enzymes that boost digestion and fight chronic disease.

Soybean: A type of bean that is high in protein. Edamame, miso, soy sauce, tempeh, and tofu are made from soybeans.

Seitan (say-tan; "tan" rhymes with "man"): Made from wheat flour or vital wheat gluten, seitan can be cooked to approximate the look, texture, and taste of meat.

Speciesism: A prejudice or bias against other beings, simply on account of their species.

Tempeh (tem-pay): A food product made from fermented soybeans.

Tofu (toh-foo): A food product made from soybeans. Also known as bean curd.

Vegan: Two of the most common reasons that people become vegans are for health and/or ethics. A person who is vegan for health reasons does not eat animals or animal products (including chicken, fish, beef, pork, milk, eggs, and cheese). A person who is vegan for ethical reasons does not eat or use animals or animal products (including for clothing, skincare products, and furnishings) and does not support the use of animals for entertainment (including zoos, circuses, marine parks, and aquariums) or research and testing.

Veganize: Term used to make a traditional animal-based dish into one that excludes any animal products.

Vegetarian: A person who does not eat the meat of animals, but does consume the milk and eggs of animals or products made with them (such as cheese).

Vigil: An activity to raise awareness in which animal rights activists and other volunteers show love and compassion towards animals as they arrive to a slaughterhouse. Vigils are often held just outside and right before animals enter. Volunteers provide water to animals and share their experiences on social media in an effort to show that animals feel pain, sadness, and suffering.

Vitamin B12: Originates from bacteria (not plants or animals) and is made by tiny one-celled microbes that are in the air, earth, and water.

Whole-food plant-based (WFPB): Whole food describes natural foods that are not heavily processed. That means whole, unrefined, or minimally refined ingredients. Plant-based means food that comes from plants and doesn't include animal ingredients such as meat, milk, eggs, or honey.

Acknowledgements

The initial concept of *Going Vegan 4 Goodness* was first conceived while I was living on a small island in the Philippines called Siargao. Due to the unexpected COVID-19 restrictions, I settled comfortably alongside a flowing river and deep within nature, a peaceful setting that was perfect for starting this book.

I'm thankful to all of my Tawin Homestay neighbors and friends, farming pals, and surfer buds. You gave me sparks of determination that I needed to get this thing rolling. Being surrounded within my Filipino roots helped to inspire my thoughts and fuel the drive to write many of the words in this book. I learned so much from all of you. Thank you.

To Michael, my identical twin brother, I'm so grateful for you and your family's support all through the years. To my mom Violeta and dad Peter, words cannot express my gratitude for you both. Thank you for instilling kindness and compassion into me and Michael.

Thank you to everyone who actively takes a stand against animal cruelty and exploitation. The world is a better place thanks to you. You have led the way with your courage and your vision for a less cruel world. Thank you for inspiring me to contribute my own message of *Going Vegan 4 Goodness*.

Thank you to my good friend and Plant-Based Nutritionist/Chef Linus Skaring for going over the health facts and figures in this book. I look forward to us getting more Thai food, tattoos, and beer, in no particular order.

Much appreciation to the professional editorial team, Kali Browne, Tracy Tuttle, and Charles Fyffe. Kali, thank you for your formatting and copy editing work. I couldn't have completed this whole vegan enchilada without your patience, guidance, and humor. Tracy, thank you for copy editing, copy writing, and formatting final touches. Your contribution and background in plant-based eating has been valuable in completing this book. Charles, thanks for giving your time to share your insight. I'm grateful for an editor who is just as passionate about the health, animal, and human rights issues related to this topic.

To all of the vegan chefs who agreed to include one of your delicious dishes in this book, I thank you for your recipe contribution and for sharing your culinary greatness. Thank you to Susan Pratt, Safiya Robinson, Lauren Toyota, Mike Sincere and Jezzy B, Erin Ireland, Del Sroufe, Haile Thomas, Linus Skaring, Charlie Fyffe, Miyoko Schinner, Rip Esselstyn, and Erika Hazel.

Thank you to my friends who uplifted me with encouragement and showed interest in the creative process of this book. A special thanks to Jay Magpantay who helped mentor and inspire me to start writing this book. I'm thankful to the Universe for connecting us that one fine day in San Diego, California. Cheers, brother!

Finally, I wish to offer a heartfelt thank you to the late animal rights activist, Regan Russell and her family. You have inspired many with your passion and bravery to rise up for what you believe in. We will always remember the goodness in your heart and what you have done for the animals and the world.

References

Preface

1. https://www.podiatrytoday.com/closer-look-mortality-after-lower-extremity- amputation
   *Actual reference: 1. Jupiter DC, Thorud JC, Buckley CJ, Shibuya N. The impact of foot ulceration and amputation on mortality in diabetic patients. I: From ulceration to death, a systematic review. Int Wound J. 2016;13(5):892-903.
2. https://www.idf.org/aboutdiabetes/what-is-diabetes/facts-figures.html

Introduction

1. https://www.asean-endocrinejournal.org/index.php/JAFES/article/view/ 267/667 (Under section: What characterizes diabetes among Asians, among Filipinos
   *Referenced: 13. Fojas MC, Lantion-Ang FL, Jimeno CA, Santiago D, Arroyo M, Laurel A, Sy H, See J. Complications and cardiovascular risk factors among newly-diagnosed type 2 diabetics in Manila. Philipp J Intern Med. 2009;47(3):99-105.)
2. https://www.ncbi.nlm.nih.gov/pmc/articles/PMC3068646/#:~:text=Diabetes%20is%20a%20major%20public,increasing%20at%20an%20alarming% 20rat e.
3. https://www.cdc.gov/diabetes/library/features/truth-about-prediabetes.html
4. https://www.un.org/en/chronicle/article/lifestyle-diseases-access-chronic-disease-care - low- and-middle-income-countries
5. https://www.cdc.gov/chronicdisease/resources/infographic/chronic-diseases.htm

Section 3 - Human Health Consequences Of Factory Farming

1. Food and Drug Administration. (2015). 2014 Summary Report on Antimicrobials Sold or Distributed for Use in Food-Producing Animals. Department of Health and Human Services. https://www.fda.gov/media/94906/download
2. https://www.cdc.gov/drugresistance/pdf/threats-report/2019-ar-threats-report-508.pdf
3. Centers for Disease Control and Prevention. (2018). Burden of Foodborne Illness: Findings https://www.cdc.gov/foodborneburden/2011-foodborne-estimates.html
4. N. Murphy, A. Knuppel, N. Papadimitriou, R. M. Martin, K. K. Tsilidis, K. Smith-Byrne, G. Fensom, A. Perez-Cornago, R. C. Travis, T.J. Key & M. J. Gunter 2020, 'Insulin-like growth factor-1, insulin-like growth factor-binding protein-3, and breast cancer risk: observational and Mendelian randomization analyses with w430 000 women', Annals Of Oncology, Volume31, Issue 5, P641-649.

Factory Farms - breeding grounds for Zoonotic Diseases

5. United States Department of Agriculture. (2019). 2017 Census Of Agriculture. United States Summary and State Data Volume 1 Geographic Area Series Part 51 (AC-17- A-51) https://www.nass.usda.gov/Publications/AgCensus/2017/Full_Report/ Volume_1,_Chapter_1_US/usv1.pdf
6. UNEP (2016). UNEP Frontiers 2016 Report: Emerging Issues of Environmental Concern. United Nations Environment Programme, Nairobi.

Farm houses are horror houses

6. Food and Agriculture Organization of the United Nations (FAO), World Health Organization (WHO), and World Organization for Animal Health (OIE) (2004). Report of the WHO/FAO/OIE joint consultation on emerging zoonotic diseases. World Health Organization, Geneva.
7. Berger, Kevin (2020, March 12). The Man Who Saw the Pandemic Coming. Nautilus. Retrieved from http://nautil.us/issue/83/intelligence/the-man-who-saw-the-pandemic- coming

Section 4 - For Our Planet and Her Inhabitants

1. J. Poore, T. Nemecek 2018 'Reducing food's environmental impacts through producers and consumers', Science, Vol. 360, Issue 6392, pp. 987-992.
2-4 Climate Nexus (2020). Animal Agriculture's Impact on Climate Change. Retrieved from https://climatenexus.org/climate-issues/food/animal-agricultures-impact-on-climate- change/
5. Rinkesh (2020). 70+ Breathtaking Facts About Deforestation That Will Leave You Spellbound [Blog post] Retrieved from https://www.conserve-energy-future.com/various- deforestation-facts.php
6. J. Poore, T. Nemecek 2018 'Reducing food's environmental impacts through producers and consumers', Science, Vol. 360, Issue 6392, pp. 987-992.
7. Union of Concerned Scientists (2016, February 8). What's Driving Deforestation? [Blog Post] Retrieved from https://www.ucsusa.org/resources/whats-driving-deforestation

8. https://www.worldwildlife.org/magazine/issues/summer-2018/articles/what-are-the- biggest-drivers-of-tropical-deforestation

Section 5 - Social Impact
1. Yazd S., Wheeler, S., Zuo, A. (2019, December 2). 'Key Risk Factors Affecting Farmers' Mental Health: A Systematic Review', International Journal of Environmental Research and Public Health, Retrieved from https://www.ncbi.nlm.nih.gov/pmc/articles/ PMC6926562/pdf/ ijerph-16-04849.pdf
2. Hoekstra, Arjen Y., (2012, April). 'The hidden water resource use behind meat and dairy', Animal Frontiers, Vol. 2, No. 2.
3. People For The Ethical Treatment of Animals (2020) 'How Much Water Does It Take to Make One Steak?', [Blog Post] Retrieved from https://www.peta.org/videos/meat-wastes- water/

Section 6 - Human Health & Wellness
1. Loria, J., (2017, January 19). 'Here Are the Top 10 Health Concerns Linked to Meat' [Blog Post] Retrieved from https://mercyforanimals.org/here-are-the-top-10- health-concerns-linked
2. U.S. Department of Agriculture (USDA), U.S. Department of Health and Human Services. Dietary Guidelines for Americans 2010. U.S. Government Printing Office, December 2010.
3. Bhaskaran K, Douglas I, Forbes H, dos-Santos-Silvia I, Leon DA, Smeeth L. "Body- Mass Index and Risk of 22 Specific Cancers: A Population-Based Cohort Study of 5.34 Million UK Adults." The Lancet 2014, vol. 384, pp. 755-765.
4. Xu J, Kochanek KD, Murphy SL, Arias E. NCHS Data Brief: Mortality in the United States, 2012. Accessed here on November 3, 2014.
5. World Health Organization (2017, May 17). Cardiovascular diseases (CVDs) Retrieved from https://www.who.int/en/news-room/fact-sheets/detail/cardiovascular-diseases-(cvds)
   ### The (Detrimental) Power of Food
6. Poore, Joseph & Nemecek, Thomas. (2018). Reducing food's environmental impacts through producers and consumers. Science (New York, N.Y.). 360. 987-992. 10.1126/ science.aaq0216
7. Centers for Disease Control and Prevention (2020) Chronic Disease. National Center for Chronic Disease Prevention and Health Promotion. Retrieved from https:// www.cdc.gov/ chronicdisease/ index.htm
8. Statista (2019, December 10). Estimated number of diabetics worldwide in 2019 and 2045. Retrieved from https://www.statista.com/statistics/271442/number-of-diabetics- worldwide/
   ### Digestion Matters
9. Suttie, J., (2012, June 27). Better Eating through Mindfulness. Greater Good Magazine Science-Based Insights for a Meaningful Life. Retrieved fromhttps://greatergood.berkeley.edu/ article/item/ better_eating_through_mindfulness
10. Suttie, J., (2012, June 27). Better Eating through Mindfulness. Greater Good Magazine Science-Based Insights for a Meaningful Life. Retrieved fromhttps://greatergood.berkeley.edu/ article/item/ better_eating_through_mindfulness

Section 7 - What is a Vegan Diet? Plant Milks
1. https://www.ncbi.nlm.nih.gov/pmc/articles/PMC2100124/
2. https://academic.oup.com/ije/advance-article-abstract/doi/10.1093/ije/ dyaa007/5743492? redirectedFrom=fulltext
   Gary E Fraser, Karen Jaceldo-Siegl, Michael Orlich, Andrew Mashchak, Rawiwan Sirirat, Synnove Knutsen, Dairy, soy, and risk of breast cancer: those confounded milks, International Journal of Epidemiology, dyaa007, https://doi.org/10.1093/ije/ dyaa007
3. Goldfarb M. Relation of time of introduction of cow milk protein to an infant and risk of type 1 diabetes mellitus. J Proteome Research. 2008;7:2165-2167.
4. Bamini Gopinath, Victoria M. Flood, Annette Kifley, Jimmy C. Y. Louie, Paul Mitchell, Association Between Carbohydrate Nutrition and Successful Aging Over 10 Years, The Journals of Gerontology: Series A, Volume 71, Issue 10, October 2016, Pages 1335– 1340, https://doi.org/10.1093/gerona/glw091
5. Xu H, Li S, Song X, Li Z, Zhang D. Exploration of the association between dietary fiber intake and depressive symptoms in adults. Nutrition. 2018 Oct;54:48-53. doi: 10.1016/j.nut.2018.03.009. Epub 2018 Mar 21. PMID: 29747090.
6. Evans Kreider K, Pereira K, Padilla BI. Practical Approaches to Diagnosing, Treating and Preventing Hypoglycemia in Diabetes. Diabetes Ther. 2017;8(6):1427-1435. doi: 10.1007/s13300-017-0325-9

7. Samantha L. Nabb & David Benton (2006) The effect of the interaction between glucose tolerance and breakfasts varying in carbohydrate and fibre on mood and cognition, Nutritional Neuroscience, 9:3-4, 161-168, DOI:10.1080/10284150600955099

Section 9 - Plant Protein
1. https://drc.bmj.com/content/bmjdrc/6/1/e000534.full.pdf
   Disease Prevention and Reversal https:// www .ncbi .nlm .nih .gov /pubmed / 22709768
2. King DE, Mainous AG 3rd, Lambourne CA. Trends in dietary fiber intake in the United States, 1999-2008. J Acad Nutr Diet. 2012;112(5):642-648. doi:10.1016/j.jand.2012.01. 019

Section 16 - Resources
1. National Institute of Diabetes and Digestive and Kidney Diseases (2017, August). Overweight & Obesity Statistics. Retrieved from https ://www .niddk .nih.gov/ health- information/health-statistics/overweight-obesity?dkrd=hispt0880
2. Origin of atherosclerosis in childhood and adolescence, The American Journal of Clinical Nutrition, Volume 72, Issue 5, November 2000, Pages 1307s-1315s, https:// doi.org/10.1093/ajcn/72.5.1307s
3. Petersen, KF M.D., Dufour, S Ph.D., Befroy, D Ph.D., Garcia, R B.A., and Shulman, GI M.D., Ph.D., (2004, February 12). 'Impaired Mitochondrial Activity in the Insulin-Resistant Offspring of Patients with Type 2 Diabetes', The New England Journal of Medicine 2004;350:664-71.<https://www.nejm.org/doi/pdf/10.1056/NEJMoa031314>
4. Physicians' Committee for Responsible Medicine (2020). Lowering Cholesterol With a Plant-Based Diet. Retrieved from https://www.pcrm.org/good-nutrition/nutrition- information/lowering-cholesterol-with-a-plant-based-diet
5. GMO Inside (2013, July 16). 'How Pervasive are GMOs in Animal Feed?' Retrieved from https://www.greenamerica.org/blog/how-pervasive-are-gmos-animal-feed
6. The Nutrition Source Harvard T.H. Chan (2020). 'Types of Fat'. Retrieved from https://www.hsph.harvard.edu/nutritionsource/what-should-you-eat/fats-and-cholesterol/types- of-fat/
7. United States Department of Agriculture (2014, September). 'Determining U.S. Milk Quality Using Bulk-Tank Somatic Cell Counts, 2013'. Retrieved from https://www.aphis.usda.gov/animal_health/nahms/dairy/downloads/dairy_monitoring/ BTSCC_2013infosheet.pdf

Photo by: Siwinat Phongboonkoomlarp
Location: Krabi, Thailand

Mark Suarkeo is the content creator of goingvegan4goodness.com, an online resource for those interested in making a plant-based lifestyle change. After working at UCLA Medical Center's Prosthetics and Orthotics Department for eleven years, he relocated to his father's home country of Thailand. During the three years that he lived in Phuket and Chiang Mai, Mark swapped out his lab coat and Allen wrenches for an apron and cooking utensils. It was during this time that he learned how to cook Thai vegan food using organically grown ingredients that came straight from his father's home farm.

In 2020, Mark lived in Siargao, Philippines for almost a year. While exploring his mother's Filipino roots, he learned how to cook plant-based Filipino food with a local farm that promotes sustainability in agriculture and food security. In early 2021, Mark went back into the prosthetics and orthotics field where he now specializes in providing care for children.